REFL
AWAKENIN
FOR SPIRIT

"Awakening and Maturity invites us to consider a heartful exploration of the inner life. Genjo Marinello shows us the importance of spiritual friendship without skipping the shadows. This book is a must read for anyone hoping to fully explore what a spiritual life can look like in our time and place."

James Ishmael Ford, author of *Introduction to Zen Koans* and
If You're Lucky, Your Heart Will Break

"This brave book is about what it means to practice Zen in our world today. A wonderful book!"

Roshi Joan Halifax, Founder, Abbot, and Head Teacher of
Upaya Institute and Zen Center, Santa Fe, New Mexico

"This little book takes us on quite an amazing journey with an American Zen priest who is willing to share everything. You will feel you are by his side all the way, surviving with him the early traumas of his life, experiencing his path to the priesthood, and coming away deeply grateful for his insights into the nature of things. I know no book on Zen that is as personal, and as captivating, as this."

Glenn Taylor (Kangan) Webb is a retired professor of East Asian
art history and religion.

"This well-written book, by a person whom I admire and respect, explores the role of spiritual companions on the journey to find peace with our un-peacefulness. Reading his thoughtful and articulate reflections has encouraged me to again notice the impact of those teachers and spiritual friends I've met along the way, who have taught me so much about how to be—and also how not to be."

Claude AnShin Thomas, Abbot of The Magnolia Zen Center,
author of *At Hell's Gate* and *Bringing Meditation to Life*

"This book is a boldly authentic journey into psychic and spiritual maturity. It is written with respect for the disciplines both of science and of mysticism. In profoundly juxtaposing the paths of Zen Buddhism and Christianity, Genjo Marinello opens many new and helpful insights into the spiritual path, among them ways of meditation and prayer."

Sister Ellen Stephen, OSH

"It is with much pleasure that I endorse this book. Genjo is a deep thinker, and profoundly curious about what this life is. His grasp of Zen, its practice and history, is impressive, and he writes about it in a clear and accessible fashion. Read the book...then read it again! Many treasures to be found."

Fred Davis, MD

"This book cuts like a surgeon's knife to the marrow of humanity's soul. Through his personal journey, Genjo reveals how our deepest and darkest capacity for malevolence lives right next door to a spirit able to practically burst with love for life and everything and everyone in it.

In this unique book, we ride on Genjo's back through years of encounters with spiritual mentors and companions, as his own psychotherapeutic process becomes a form of self-therapy for us."

Jeff Chozen Skolnick, MD, PhD
Author of *Blessed by Distress* and *Awaken Your Brain*

"A compelling account of spiritual and psychological liberation paid for in sweat and tears over a lifetime of exertion. Measuring wealth as experience, this book is a gift of gold. With openhearted generosity, Marinello shares the harvest of a lifetime of searching, anchored in rigorous Zen training, refined through unflinching psychological self-examination, and enriched by Christian mysticism. He then presents, by example, the way that all true wisdom must show itself: through compassionate action. This is an account aglow with the uncompromising honesty demanded for awakening and with the spirit of generous service by which all true wisdom must reveal itself."

Bodhin Kjolhede is the Abbot and Director of the Rochester Zen Center, and a Dharma successor of Roshi Philip Kapleau.

"This book is a luminous guide for those who wish to show up with full presence to companion others on the path to awakening, and thereby deepen their own journey of authentic being. The section that compares the legendary Zen Ox pictures with Teresa of Avila's mystical masterpiece, The Interior Castle, moved me deeply. I never imagined how precisely these two maps for navigating the inner life would complement and enhance one another, activating the beauty and potency of both teachings in an entirely fresh and relevant way."

Mirabai Starr, Translator of Teresa of Avila
and author of *Wild Mercy*

"I read once that a koan is 'an anecdote used to provoke enlightenment.' I would describe Genjo Marinello's book as a koan of insight and inspiration gleaned from his life story. Using the metaphors of nature and nurture he bravely and compassionately shares his life story and the spiritual awakening and maturity that comes from the willingness to openly and gently step into your own life. His description of the spiritual life as not linear but more like an 'expanding lumpy spiral' invites each one of us to follow the path of our own lumpy spirals!"

Lucy Abbott Tucker is the author of Spiritual Direction
Supervision: Principles, Practices and Storytelling
Through Genjo's compelling narrative, this wise and humble

teacher reminds us that becoming spiritually mature is a continual commitment to both awakening spiritually and maturing psychologically. While it's tempting to assume that the more we awaken spiritually the more we grow psychologically, this book offers a much needed reality check. With candor and concreteness, Genjo recounts the ongoing psychological challenges he has navigated and witnessed as a Zen priest and spiritual leader. Thank you Genjo for this masterful interweaving of insights from Eastern and Western wisdom with your lived experience. I highly recommended this thought-provoking, soul-stirring book to spiritual directors and all those who want to learn more about psycho-spiritual unfolding.

Diane M. Millis, PhD, Educator, Spiritual Director, and Author of *Re-Creating a Life*

"I had no idea Genjo had such an amazing and rich background. This book was a wonderful trip for me. I even had a "mini-enlightenment" along the way."

Leonard Shaw, MSW , Author of *Love and Forgiveness*

REFLECTIONS ON
AWAKENING & MATURITY
FOR SPIRITUAL COMPANIONS

GENJO MARINELLO

2021

SDI PRESS
BELLEVUE, WASHINGTON, USA

Published by SDI Press, a division of Spiritual Directors International, 2025 112th Ave NE, Suite #200, Bellevue, WA 98004 USA.

www.sdicompanions.org
ISBN: 978-1-950309-02-3

Photos: Chobo-Ji Zen Temple collection

Cover design and book layout: Matthew Whitney

The ox-herding paintings presented in this book are by the Japanese painter Gyokusei Jikihara Sensei (1904-2005) who painted them while in residence at New York's Zen Mountain Monastery in 1982. The images are reprinted here with permission from the Monastery.

Acknowledgements

I could not have written this book, in fact I might not be alive in human form, if it weren't for the love and support of my life partner and best friend, Carolyn Josen Stevens. We live and work together in our one-bedroom apartment with our dog Charlie at the Chobo-Ji Zen Residential Practice Center. She has been one of my most important sounding boards throughout this process. My first draft was four times the length of this offering, and Rev. Seifu Singh-Molares helped me realize that perhaps I had already written three or four books. He helped me sort out what would work best for the spiritual companion audience. My principal editors have been Rev. Anne Sendo Howells, who methodically went through the first and final drafts, and Bob Daigan Timmer who went through the third draft, an exacting editor who also helped me see the missing transitions needed to pull this book together. Finally, I want to thank all my spiritual companions, many more than could fit in this first offering, who have nurtured and supported me on my life journey, including my now adult daughter Adrienne Pasta. I've often said that the dynamics of a healthy marriage are the best therapy anyone can find, and raising a child is the most significant catalyst for one's own growth and development.

CONTENTS

FOREWORD

The cover of this book is meant to invoke the Japanese art of Kintsugi ("golden joinery"), a process whereby broken items are carefully seamed back together with gold. The results are prized for their aesthetic value, as a celebration of "wabi-sabi," or the inherent beauty in the flaws and imperfections of an object. But the concept extends more broadly into a generalized acceptance of impermanence, imbued with serene melancholy and spiritual longing.

What a perfect analogy for anyone on a spiritual path!

In this book, Genjo Marinello reveals his own journey through brokenness and repair, bravely and generously, allowing us all to read ourselves into him. After all, who among us hasn't struggled with trauma and loss? And despair when we can't seem to find our way through?

All of this is the province of spiritual companions, and Genjo expertly shows us how to move forward, not just through his insights as a long time spiritual director, but also in his roles as a psychotherapist, and, perhaps most significantly, as a Zen Master (or "Roshi"). Who better to help us discern our path than someone who has dedicated his life to doing his own deep work for the sake of others?

The book chronicles this lifelong and ongoing commitment, through thick and thin, as well as a courageous embrace of many difficulties, shortcomings and flaws.

1

Genjo composts all of these into assets, establishing them as the building blocks for his own ongoing spiritual growth and evolution. And by extension, for ours.

In the process, he engages with numerous spiritual companions and models, most notably the Buddha, St Teresa of Avila, and the Zen Oxherding pictures. They reveal insights and challenges both easy and joyful, along with some quite hard and painful.

As Genjo often says, "every day is a new beginning," and a new opportunity for us to become our better selves. But that doesn't mean it's going to be easy.

Indeed, one of the more arresting conclusions of the book is that even after we awaken spiritually, we are all still a mixed bag, with shining moments, less flattering ones, and some where we fall far short of the mark. Awakening, he argues, does not mean spiritual maturity, as counterintuitive as this may seem.

So, we get on with the hard work of continuously reconstructing ourselves, with our wounds and scars acknowledged and visible to us and to our spiritual companions, who help support us, gently and tenderly, as we rebuild ourselves from our broken constituent pieces.

This book is itself a loving form of spiritual companionship, as Genjo shares his story and becomes a model for us all in how to turn pain, loss and trauma into the necessary fertilizer for spiritual growth and maturity.

Rev. Seifu Anil Singh-Molares
Executive Director, SDI

2

PREFACE

The path towards individuation, awakening and maturity is impossible without companions. For better and worse our maturation depends on our relationship to significant family members, teachers, and mentors. If we are lucky, we will find spiritual guides that mirror our shortcomings, are honest about their own, and point the way towards tapping wisdom and expressing compassion. A big part of any spiritual companion relationship is assessing where we are in our own unfolding spiritual journey, where we have been and where we may need to deepen or explore.

This book chronicles a bit of what I've learned from knowing and working with my most prominent spiritual companions during 65 orbits around the sun. Though I introduce many of them, and share some anecdotes about my journeys with them, mostly I share how these encounters became stepping-stones in the unfolding journey of my life. Each deep human encounter becomes a catalyst for our growth. This book reveals some of the lessons I've gleaned along the Way. Some insights arose from the briefest of encounters. Some insights arose from deep investigation of ancient masters long dead. Many of the lessons herein arose from hitting the rocks of immaturity hidden in myself and in the spiritual teachers with whom I have associated deeply. No one can grow and learn for us; however, our teachers may suggest what to explore, and may point to what we can't know but can learn to feel. What they mustn't do is give us the answers we are looking for. On the other hand, there is no harm done when our teachers leave cairns along the paths they have explored so that we may explore them for ourselves.

Most everything herein is derived from ancient wisdom about spiritual development readily found in Zen and Christian perspectives. I will spend time investigating the difference between the process of spiritual awakening and deep maturity. Can there be awakening without maturity? Yes! Awakening alone is only a foothold on the endless path of maturation. If we aren't always beginning just where we are, we have been sidetracked into arrogance, ignorance or spiritual bypassing.

When does our unique path of individual awakening begin? Undoubtedly it must be in utero. Brain activity begins at eight weeks. Was our first conscious sensation awareness of our mother's beating heart? What was our first thought? What was our first feeling? Before any sense of self or other were we bathed in love? Our first caretaker and mentor is our mother. Her love need not have been unconditional, but with any luck it was good enough to be both physically and spiritually nurturing. As we grew and matured towards our own birth were the limitations of the womb becoming restrictive? Perhaps we longed to be let out of Eden?

EARLY DAYS...

I was born November 5, 1954 in North Hollywood, California to parents who were both married to other people at the time of my birth. My mother, Maureen Dawn O'Shea, was only 19 and my father, Joe Marinello, was 31. The first few months of my life were rather blissful living at my maternal grandparents' house in the San Fernando Valley. I'm told the family's German Shepherd was my constant companion and slept under my crib at night. My grandparents had a pool, and there are pictures of me, as an infant, swimming before I could walk. My passion for swimming has never left me. I am like a fish in water and love to snorkel. From a young age, I wanted to learn to fly so I could move in the air with the same freedom I felt swimming under water. I could never understand why in elementary school my swimming teachers insisted that I learn how to swim on top of the water; I thought, "how boring."

After my parents separated from their previous partners they moved in together. I was three months old. My father was a brute and beat me nearly every night for disturbing his sleep until I was mostly "potty trained" at a year and a half. My mother said I screamed until I lost my breath. She cried and screamed too, but to no avail because she was afraid to leave. Later, when I wasn't waking up my parents regularly in the night, my mother found her courage and told my father if he didn't stop beating me, she would leave him. So, he mostly left me alone the rest of my life. As you might imagine, this early history has had a monumental impact on my whole life, much of it necessarily devoted to processing this early trauma. At 65 I think most of this karmic history has been combusted or composted, but I doubt all of it will be processed before I die.

My early relationship with my parents was far from all pain and sorrow. For example, because of my dyslexia I couldn't read at grade level until my senior year of high school and then only much more slowly than others, but my mother gladly and warmly read for me everything I needed to read and learn until then. As a young child I always felt free to climb into her lap for comfort. Without this kind of love early in life I surely would not be here. My father stayed distant but provided adequately for the family, though he had a hard time keeping a job for long because of his violent temper. When I was in the third grade about a half-dozen sixth graders had decided I was an easy target for bullying and would stand behind a fence and jump me on my way home from school and give this momma's boy a beating. This went on for several days without abatement. My maternal grandmother tried to put an end to it by scolding the boys on the street where they lived, which of course only made things worse. My father heard about this and insisted that I fight back. I cried that I couldn't because I was so frightened and outnumbered, and he slapped me hard across the face. Over the weekend he forced me to spar with him and to practice throwing punches at a mattress he put up against a wall. When Monday came, I put my lunch box down and put up my fists just before I knew the boys behind the corner fence would jump me. Sure enough, once again they beat me up pretty good, but this time I fought back hard and got in few good licks. Unbeknownst to me my father and his best friend, who was like an uncle to me, sat and watched in a car across the street. (I didn't learn of this for more than twenty years.) The next day I put down my lunch box once again, but no one was waiting behind the fence and the boys never bullied me again. Without my father's mentoring I might not have learned to never give up even when facing impossible odds, and that to fail and lose was much better than to never have tried.

My mother never completed high school; my father never made it past the ninth grade. My maternal grandfather abandoned his wife and children in Los Angeles when my mother was four years old, and she and her younger sister ended up in foster care with sexual abusers. My maternal grandmother remarried a medical student when my mother was a young teenager. My step-grandfather, Dr. Beverly Owens, was the only grandfather I ever knew. He became a General Practice physician and much later in life a psychiatrist and chief medical officer of Folsom Prison. Though both he and my maternal grandmother were alcoholics, I received much love and attention from them both. I consider my grandfather to be my first mentor outside of my parent's governance. Because of my mother's insistence and my grandfather's constant love and attention, I always knew I would be the first among all my cousins to go to college.

As a young child I was taught to say my prayers at night. Both my parents were lapsed Catholics. My mother later told me that I was baptized Roman Catholic just in case. She saw how fervent my prayers were and made a conscious decision to keep me from the church for fear I would become a priest. (After I shaved my head to become a Buddhist priest, she said that at least if she had let me go to church, I would still have my hair.) My father believed all religions were just a crutch to deal with uncertainty and the unknown. I went to church with other family members and friends but grew up sharing my father's view of religion. Nevertheless, throughout my conscious life I've never lost a sense that we are all a part of something vast and wondrous. I continued to investigate, "What is *this*?"

By high school I was convinced that only science could possibly explain the universe. When I was in junior high, I discovered astronomy, and while other kids were at parties in high school, I was going to all night star parties to view the heavens, far from L.A.'s city lights, with my 10-inch Newtonian Reflector telescope. There, looking at the heavenly wonders, I asked myself, why is it all here and what is our place in this vast expanse? I also made regular trips to the Griffith Observatory, where I first learned of pulsars, quasars, black holes and Einstein's special and general relativity from the observatory director, Dr. William Kaufmann. I was seriously hooked, planned to major in astronomy in college and even taught a short astronomy course as a senior in high school. I have sustained my interest in astronomy and cosmology to this day. Often, on clear nights I may be found up on the rooftop of our Zen residential practice center taking photos of planets, nebulas, star clusters and galaxies.

Because of lack of accommodations for my dyslexia my SAT scores were low. Rather than apply to schools where I had little chance of being accepted, I opted to attend the local community college. There I met one of the most influential mentors and spiritual companions of my life, my freshman English professor, Jim Chambers. I was not able to get into freshman English my first semester because I failed the entrance exam. As I recall I failed primarily because I could not identify the misspelled words in a paragraph. I was forced to take remedial English. This was a good review but did nothing to improve my atrocious spelling, so I failed the English entrance exam a second time. Undaunted, I "ran" for freshman English by getting a professor to sign me into class after registration was closed; that professor was Jim Chambers. His approach to freshman English completely changed the course of my life. Mr. Chambers taught what he called the "Classic

Humanistic Tradition." We read Dostoevsky, Ibsen, Arthur Miller, Kafka, Sinclair Lewis and others. We also read the Sermon at Benares by Siddhartha Gautama, which was my first introduction to Buddhism, and the Sermon on the Mount by Jesus of Nazareth. Mr. Chambers asked us the most amazing questions: Where did these authors get their inspiration to write about the human condition? How do scientists come to their insights about the nature of reality? Do the sages of world religions tap some innate source of wisdom? In a way these questions have become my life's quest and I will be forever grateful to Mr. Chambers for posing them. After freshman English many of his students would meet at his house to discuss these and other pressing questions. He provided us with an extracurricular reading list, which we all devoured. I believe it was then that I was first introduced to the writings of Erich Fromm and Karen Horney. Fromm's *You Shall Be as Gods* and Horney's *Our Inner Conflicts* moved me towards the study of psychology and my own psyche. This was also the time when I read (from cover to cover) my family's *King James Bible*, the *Koran*, the *Dhammapada*, the *Bhagavad Gita*, the *Tao Tei Ching*, the *I Ching* and other sacred texts. I came to the impression that though these texts were from different cultures, times and religions, they were very likely inspired from the same well of deep insight. I kept in contact with my third mentor, Jim Chambers, for many years after graduating.

During my first year at community college my father

was thinking of moving the family to Detroit to pursue an entrepreneurial sales position where he thought he could make a lot of money. The idea of moving across the country really depressed me. I was so distressed that I did not do well my first semester, but being the nerd that I am I escaped by immersing myself in a computer programming course and lost myself in writing code. (Sometimes it was so complicated that it would freeze the whole Los Angeles community college computer system.) This passion for coding never left me, and after college I spun this passion into a software company called Satori Software. This venture was successful enough to put me through graduate school and allowed me to pursue and gain my private pilot's license and the purchase of a single engine airplane. (Today I still fly, and I manage my temple's web presence.) When my father's plans fell through, I ended up retaking two courses my second semester, and after two years transferred to UCLA.

Four courses at UCLA deeply influenced my worldview. One was a course on anthropology where I gained an appreciation for the deep wisdom and compassion that can be found in most indigenous cultures. One book associated with this course profoundly moved me, *Freedom and Culture* by Dorothy Lee. The second was a course in learning theory where I learned about the difference between hardwired instincts and predispositions and the flexibility that allows us to make associations across brain schema. The teacher, Professor

John Garcia, had humble roots. He was born near Santa Rosa, California to a farm family and he died in 2012, a world-renowned member of the National Academy of Sciences. Of my UCLA professors, Dr. Garcia stands out most in my mind. I will never forget his down to earth clarity and passion for learning theory. The third course was on evolution where I wrote a paper titled "Naturalistic Vitalism." In this paper I argued that Darwin was not a hyper-materialist and showed that his writings left room for what we call God as the First Cause. I ventured that when "enough matter comes together in a highly organized form" what we think of as mind becomes evident in the same way that gravity becomes evident when matter is concentrated enough. Whatever gave birth to the universe became the fabric of the natural laws that govern the development of matter, stars, planets, life and consciousness. In other words, the universe by its nature was destined from the moment of the Big Bang to become conscious of itself and curious about the unknowable First Cause.

For me the most important course I took at UCLA was on Eastern religions. I took this course in my junior year. This is when I first read *What the Buddha Taught* by Walpola Rahula. I must have underlined half the lines in this book (*Buddha* means "awakened one"). Around this time, I also picked up a paperback copy of *Zen Flesh Zen Bones* by Paul Reps and Nyogen Senzaki and found myself mystified by Zen *koans*, which are tantalizing parables and pithy exchanges between ancient Zen masters. It was during this year that I met my next mentor and spiritual companion, Brian Daizen Victoria, a Soto Zen priest who was at that time a UCLA graduate student in East Asian studies.

I first saw Daizen, who always dressed in Zen robes on campus, rolling around on the grass laughing with hundreds of other students at our resident foul-mouthed comic sage and holy fool, Swami X. Swami X told us he had attained the full wisdom of the East on the streets of Brooklyn New York. In his stand-up routines atop a soapbox, Swami X attacked the government, the administration and all religions. The student body made vinyl recordings of him, and some of these recordings can be found today on YouTube. I thought to myself, if a Zen priest can laugh with the rest of us then this religion might be for me.

In my Eastern religions course, I had seen pictures of Zen temples and the monks who resided in them; therefore, I was confident that Daizen was indeed a Zen practitioner. Ever since Mr. Chambers had inspired me to deeply wonder where inspiration and insight come from, I had been investigating through reading and study the methods the mystics of world religions used to cultivate wisdom and understanding. I already had concluded that I would need to try Zen meditation, though the idea of deep silence prodded by inscrutable koans scared me. My mind was always racing, the idea of trying to be quiet for any length of time in order to wait for deep insight while pondering paradoxical anecdotes left me feeling inadequate. I was very dependent on and attached to my own logical reasoning, and my mind was continually analyzing the world. I knew from my reading that koans could not be penetrated with one's logical faculties. If I did Zen training, would I become psychotic and not be able to distinguish this and that, right and wrong? With my heart pounding, I needed to find out!

One day after listening to Swami X, I followed Daizen and got his attention. I asked if he would share lunch with me. Over lunch I must have talked without interruption for thirty minutes or more. All the while, Daizen ate his salad and did not say a word. When I finally paused, Daizen only said I would need to learn zazen (seated meditation). He told me he was living at the College of Oriental Studies, where the director, a Vietnamese Zen Buddhist monk by the name of Thích Thiên-Ân, taught meditation every week. I took several introductory classes with Ven. Thích Thiên-Ân and began meditating every day. I have continued to meditate nearly every day since then. He was a very kind, simple, clear and direct teacher of Zen meditation, and I will always feel fortunate to have first learned the form from him. His book *Zen Philosophy, Zen Practice* was published the year I met him and was seminal in my early understanding of Zen practice. During my remaining time at UCLA I had the good fortune of getting to know both Daizen and

Thích Thiên-Ân. I've had on-and-off contact with Daizen for many years. Daizen went on to write several books, two of which have been very close to my heart, *Zen Master Dogen: An Introduction with Selected Writings* and *Zen at War*, where Daizen chronicles the often contradictory and militaristic role of Zen Buddhism throughout World War II. Brian originally traveled to Japan as a Christian missionary, but ended up converting to Buddhism and becoming a Zen priest. My first Zen mentor was not only a Zen monk and graduate student, but also an anti-war activist who got kicked out of Japan for anti-Vietnam protests. His model of grounded meditation with social action has never left me.

I remember well one of my early meditations alone in my dorm room. After about twenty minutes my mind became eerily quiet and it felt like I had eyes in the back of my head. Even though my eyes were mostly closed, gazing gently at the floor in front of me, my perception of the world all around me was heightened. I could somehow *feel* the room and beyond as fully alive or vibrant. I thought, "What is *this*?" Fascinated and intrigued, I continue my investigation to this day. After more than 40 years of daily meditation practice, I can summarize my instructions for silent meditation as *sit, breathe and listen.* — Take a seat on a chair or a cushion, plant your tailbone like a taproot deep into mother earth, and erect the spine like an antenna to the heavens. This helps you to be aware of a nexus between heaven and earth right in your own center of gravity. From your center of gravity, breathe slow, gentle whole breaths, extending the exhalation until it is complete but not forced. Over the course of a meditation period the breath will become ever more slow, smooth, and rhythmic. With each breath, release all tension, stress, worry and concern. With each inhalation, draw up a breath of fresh new energy and spaciousness. When feeling distracted for any reason, count off ten slow exhalations. Gently and attentively listen on all channels of perception to the symphony of now. Let all thoughts, feelings and sensations come and go, like clouds passing in the sky. Try not to analyze or judge, just let go and let be, or, let go and let God. Watch for the silence, stillness, or quiet power between and within each note. This quiet power is always ready to hold and nurture us. As your heart begins to open, notice how your heart-mind is seamless with all other open heart-minds around the planet, ready to embrace this troubled world and your own trials and tribulations with loving presence.

VISTA VOLUNTEER, FIRST ZEN RETREAT & FIRST QUAKER MEETING

I graduated from UCLA in June of 1976 and immediately joined Volunteers in Service to America (VISTA), which at that time was much like the Peace Corps, only inside the United States. I got my choice of two possible assignments – an alcohol counselor in Alaska or a community organizer in the Central District of Seattle. I chose the latter. I languished a bit my first year because I had little training and felt like a fish out of water.

Nevertheless, that first year in VISTA was very significant because I met and began a relationship with a fellow volunteer, Diane Pasta. She was an attorney who was assigned to assist seniors in Seattle. We eventually became deeply and intimately involved with each other, moved into a collective house (called PRAG House – as I recall the acronym stands for People's Revolutionary Action Group) owned by the Evergreen Land Trust, and had a child together. Our daughter Adrienne was born in 1983. Near the close of my first year in VISTA,

I also began my association with my next four spiritual mentors. The first was Fr. Greg Galluzzo, a Jesuit priest at the time I knew him, and a master community organizer. (Greg in later years went on to train Barack Obama in Chicago.) Fr. Galluzzo introduced me to the very progressive Archbishop Raymond Hunthausen, who actively supported Fr. Galluzzo's work, and to his lead organizer Pete DeSilva, who became a life-long friend. I went on several protests with Archbishop Hunthausen, and shared a few dinners with him when he hosted Greg and other community organizers. He was an inspiration on so many topics close to my heart, including war tax resistance. With Greg's and Pete's encouragement and counsel, I got out on the streets of the Central District knocking door to door and was instrumental in founding the Cherry Hill Coalition, which for a time was the most powerful community-led neighborhood organization in Seattle. As part of my work, I attended nearly every black church in the Central District at least once, and developed personal relationships with many of the pastors. This opened my mind to the fact that there are many workable spiritual paths. I learned that by following Fr. Galluzzo's methods local leadership could be cultivated that would have the power to effect real change in disadvantaged neighborhoods. *Rules for Radicals: A Pragmatic Primer for Realistic Radicals* by Saul Alinsky was our organizing handbook.

Zen meditation sustained me during my three years

as a community organizer. The first six months in Seattle I could not find the location of the Seattle Zen Center (SZC), which I knew met somewhere on the University of Washington campus. Early in 1977 I did find the group, which was founded by Dr. Glenn Kangan Webb, at the time an Art History professor at the University of Washington, who had done many years of Zen training in Japan. I did my first weeklong sesshin (intensive Zen meditation retreat) with the SZC on Vashon Island, in the middle of Puget Sound, a short ferry ride from Seattle. At that time Dr. Webb invited the Soto Zen Master Hirano Katsufumi Osho-san from Japan twice a year to lead SZC sesshins.

During this retreat, Hirano Osho-san would occasionally cover the stopwatch used to time our periods of meditation with the bell that is rung to start and end a sit. When this happened all of us knew the period would be excruciatingly long, perhaps an hour or more. During one of these particularly gruesome sits I let go of my attachments to control, strength and safety. From this moment of surrender forward there was no fear. Time seemed to stop. All hope, scheming and analysis stopped. There was a kind of floating harmonious feeling of just being present. Gentle tears began to flow. I cannot say the pain diminished, but it did become distant and inconsequential. There was a profound peace and the sense of being completely at home.

When the bell rang, signaling the end of the sit, I got up to do walking meditation with the group, a practice known as *kinhin*. During the walk there was an awareness of motion, a grace that I had never felt before. Turning a corner in the meditation hall, my eyes found, through a window, a view of bright, thick, white fog mixing with an evergreen tree and grass, both dripping with dew. No words can do justice to the impact this view had upon me. I wanted to shout to my companions, "Don't you hear it? Don't you see it?" But there was nothing new to hear or see that hadn't been there all the time. A stream of gentle tears flowed down my face, and a profound joy filled my heart. From that moment my life was upended. In some unfathomable way I felt my death and rebirth. My death came as a combination of surrendering personal control over my fate and a sense of instantly dissolving and being blown away by the sight of morning fog, completely gone, yet fully awake. Rebirth came in the realization that there was still a bodily form walking around the room, but it was no longer the constructed ego identity with which I was so familiar. Who was now walking around the room? I did not know, but it felt fresh, unburdened, natural and real. I did know this much, if there were any way for me to share or assist others in feeling this loving presence emanating from everything seen and unseen, this would be the greatest of all gifts to give.

After a few more sits, where I was no longer distracted by pain or discomfort and was cruising harmoniously with the environment, I met with Hirano Osho-san and Glenn Webb. At that meeting, with Glenn translating, I asked, "What is it when the fog and trees speak, but there are no words?" Hirano said, "That's the beginning of real practice." At this point I began to seriously consider becoming a Zen *unsui* (cloud and water person – novice Zen monk).

During my last two years as a VISTA volunteer, I was living not far from the University of Washington in a collective household. One of the women who lived there regularly attended University Friends Meeting (UFM – a non-programmed Quaker Meeting). As a community organizer I was encouraged to attend churches of all denominations in the central area neighborhoods where I served. From this experience I learned that every faith tradition, Christian or otherwise, sought to connect with something beyond our narrow ego identity. I was curious how the Quakers might approach this so I tagged along with my housemate one Sunday. At the Quaker meeting nothing was said for thirty minutes; in other words, there was only silent communion with the presence of something that best remains unnamed. After thirty minutes of quiet, a couple of attendees were quaked with the spirit to rise from their seats and say something to the gathered assembly. I found "Friends," as Quaker members referred to themselves, were very progressive activists working in the world for equality and social justice. After just one meeting I realized I felt right at home. Here was a tradition where I didn't need to translate Eastern philosophy into something understandable to my Judeo-Christian upbringing. Eventually, I went on to become a Friend myself. I've tried to borrow Quaker values and methods to help shape the development of Zen in the West. In my view, all of us need to come out of our place of worship with intention and energy to bring progressive, direct, loving, action into the world. A Quaker story illustrates this: "A newcomer to meeting during the initial protracted silence asks an elder, 'when does the service begin?' The elder responds, 'After the worship.'"

I began attending the weekly Quaker meeting and all the offerings at the SZC. Dr. Webb was a qualified

Zen priest and teacher in his own right and an Urasenke Tea master to boot. However, given his university responsibilities, he could not serve as a full-time temple priest to the SCZ. Therefore, he began a search for a Zen priest from Japan who might be willing to relocate to Seattle. Glenn decided to invite Genki Takabayashi, whom he felt had potential after sitting a sesshin with him in Japan. Glenn learned that Genki had been considered a bright rising star in his lineage until some misbehavior sidelined him, severely limiting any chance that he would be allowed to advance. Genki arrived in Seattle in the late fall of 1977, and I was one of a handful of Zen students to greet him at the airport. Our small group became quickly enamored with his simple, joyful, playful, unpretentious presence. Unbeknownst to me, and almost as soon as Genki arrived, a letter came from Morinaga Roshi in Japan, expressing his deep dissatisfaction with these developments and saying that Genki should return to Japan for further disciplinary action and training (evidently Genki had gotten a neighborhood woman pregnant and then refused to marry her, which according to Japanese temple rules was the truly unforgivable part). Genki ignored this condemnation and was determined to stay in the United States. Glenn helped him to get a green card, slowly we adopted him as our temple priest, and over time we began to affectionately call him *Roshi* (Old Master).

I continued to train with and support Genki until

his death in 2013. Without a doubt Genki turned out to be one of my most influential spiritual companions. After completing three years as a VISTA volunteer and community organizer, I applied in the early summer of 1979 to become the Executive Director of the Cherry Hill Coalition, but I was not selected. This turned out to be a fortuitous event, because it gave me the time to further explore what I felt was a calling to cultivate wisdom and compassion through communion with that which best remains nameless.

There were some early warning signs that demonstrated that Genki did not have good boundaries. Many of us were falling in love with him as a teacher, and some women were falling in love with him as a man. In and of itself this was not a problem. However, Genki returned and encouraged these affections instead of holding to appropriate student-teacher boundaries. One woman left her husband to be with Genki, and her teenage son hung himself in part because of issues aggravated by his parent's divorce. Somehow this was kept secret from most everyone; I certainly didn't know anything about it, and learned of this only after Glenn published his memoir, *Sugoi Yo (OMG): Thoughts About Music, Art, Religion, People and Places in My Life*, in 2016. Today I feel I must have been very young and naïve not to have known more. Because of what we did know at that time, we warned all women to be aware that Genki might be inclined to flirt with them. We told them that it was very unusual for female students to train with male teachers in Japan, and because Japanese culture did not discourage private affairs between consenting men and women, he did not know how to hold appropriate boundaries. Genki was told repeatedly that it was inappropriate to have an affair with a Zen Center student, but this caution never seemed to get through to him. In hindsight, we were all naïve and blinded by his love of the *Dharma* (Laws of the Universe – Spiritual Truth), dazzling simplicity, sincerity and artistry as a calligrapher, master cook, gardener, and potter.

UNSUI TRAINING IN JAPAN

Not long after my VISTA contract concluded, and while I was wondering what I would do next, the Dalai Lama made his first visit to Seattle. It was in October of 1979 and Glenn Webb was one of the principal organizers of this event. Because of this association the Dalai Lama paid a visit to our small Zen group! At another point in his visit, the Dalai Lama gave a talk one evening at the University of Washington. He spoke on the Four Noble Truths originally stated by the historical Buddha, Siddhartha Gautama, in his first sermon at Deer Park in India more than 2,500 years ago. He explained these truths so clearly and simply that I was very moved. In addition, he handled communist hecklers with great care and compassion. To summarize what I recall of his talk, he related that the Four Noble Truths were much like the process a physician uses to investigate and treat disease. The physician looks at the symptoms, makes a diagnosis, offers a prognosis and then suggests a course of action hopefully leading to a cure. As the Dalai Lama put it, the First Noble Truth – the existence of *Dukkha* (suffering, struggle, sorrow) states the symptoms. The Second Noble

Truth – the arising of *Dukkha* (ignorance, attachment, repulsion) is the diagnosis of the disease. The Third Noble Truth – the cessation of *Dukkha* (enlightenment, Nirvana, Satori) is the prognosis that a cure is possible. The Fourth Noble Truth – the path that leads to the cessation of *Dukkha* (the Noble Eight-Fold Path) delineates the actions needed to effect a cure.

That night after the Dalai Lama's talk, I resolved to give myself more fully to the Buddhist path. I asked Glenn to set up a meeting with Genki. Soon the three of us met in Glenn's UW office and I explained that I would do whatever it took to give myself to this course of study. Furthermore, I told them if that meant being ordained and being sent to Japan then so be it. I was ordained as a Zen priest in training (*unsui*) on October 5, 1980 and sent to train in Japan a year later.

Because most of my training was to be in Seattle apprenticing with Genki, I was only expected to sample one winter training period at Ryutaku-Ji in Mishima, Japan as a guest. The abbot at Ryutaku-Ji was Sochu Suzuki Roshi. He was a Dharma brother of Genki Takabayashi, as they shared the same ordination teacher. Also at Ryutaku-Ji at that time was the retired abbot Soen Nakagawa Roshi. Soen Roshi was considered a national treasure, and I was very fortunate to meet and train with him briefly while in Japan.

Sometime during my second sesshin at Ryutaku-Ji I was able to satisfy Sochu Roshi in *dokusan* (one-on-one Dharma interview). Dokusan is a brief heart-mind to heart-mind encounter that rarely exceeds a couple of minutes. In dokusan one's insight about a koan is presented and tested. The koan I was working on was Joshu's *Mu* (the Chinese ideogram for the ineffable – literally translated as "no, not, or nothing"). How does one present the ineffable? When a student penetrates this or similar koans, the master is always happy. It means that the student has seen at least somewhat into their own deep nature, which from a Zen perspective is the same depth of loving presence or intimate infinite that we all share and is the very origin of creation.

Once I had satisfied Sochu Roshi in dokusan, Roshi and the other monks training at the temple were confident that I was a serious practitioner. On a few occasions, I was brought out of the temple as Sochu Roshi's assistant, especially towards the end of the calendar year when he would make visits to major temple supporters. I was expected to carry things for him, chant with him, and politely be seen but not heard. I think in part he was showing off his *gaijin* (foreigner) monk. See how he can bow, chant, sit full lotus, and use *hashi* (chopsticks). It may sound odd, but this was really my first experience of not being a part of a privileged class. All gaijin were treated with a bit of disdain and thought of as clumsy buffoons. I felt at times like a very large pet. From this experience, I began to have a bit of insight into how people of color feel in the USA.

Soen Roshi was an enigma to nearly everyone. He was a renowned *haiku* poet and Zen master who, beginning in 1949, had often traveled to the United States. During my time at Ryutaku-Ji he was a recluse and spent most of his time alone in his hermitage hut. Monks would leave food at the sliding door. When alone he would bring the tray of food inside and leave his used dishes outside the door to be retrieved. The first month I was there I never saw him, but he must have had a small TV or radio inside because I would often hear that when I was cleaning the temple near his hut.

One day Eido Tai Shimano, the abbot of Dai Bosatsu Zendo (DBZ) monastery in New York State and one of Soen's Dharma Heirs, was traveling in Japan and came to visit Soen at Ryutaku-Ji. Soen Roshi refused to see him, which felt very unusual, and I remember Eido's obvious disappointment. However, during that time period Soen Roshi refused all visitors. Soen had had a head injury in 1967 and was unconscious for three days. People close to him before and after this accident said he was never the same after that. When he felt crazy or unstable, Soen would retreat to his hut and remain a recluse until he felt better.

During *Teisho* (formal Dharma talks on a koan) given by Sochu Roshi during sesshins, I was sent to a small room positioned between the kitchen and Soen's hut to listen to cassette tapes of English teishos given by Soen Roshi. My Japanese was so poor that there was no sense sitting in on Sochu's teishos. While I sat alone in this small room, Soen Roshi walked in. He had a long beard and scraggly hair and was dressed only in a tattered, disheveled white *kimono*. My mouth dropped open, he looked at me and he too was surprised and simply said, *gassho*! (bow), which I did. Evidently, he was getting something from the kitchen and certainly did not expect me to be along his path as he returned to his hut. After this brief encounter I began to see more and more of him around the temple. He began to occasionally sit zazen with the other monks, receive visitors, make long distance calls to friends, and share meals with us. Over time, he became more aware of me, and we began to take walks together on the temple grounds. His English was excellent and we had long talks. I was completely smitten by his gentle, poetic, ordinary, generous, simple, clear and direct manner and I will always treasure this opportunity to be in his presence for a couple of months.

I learned from Soen that Zen did not need to be martial. On the other hand, I also understood that because most of the monks training at Japanese temples were the eldest sons of temple priests, monastic practice was considered their lot in life. Their fatalistic attitude meant that these young men required something like the rigor of a boot camp to learn the ornate forms and rituals. The other monks could not accept that I volunteered to train at Zen. Only when I said that my ordination teacher sent me could they make sense of my participation. I think there were about ten other monks training at Ryutaku-Ji at that time, and I must admit that the very rigorous martial attitude slowly but surely had an overall positive effect on everyone. Together we became one unit or mind that cared for the practice and the extensive temple grounds. I could feel us all shedding some of our egocentric dependencies and preferences, and very slowly becoming more simple, real and grounded, doing day after day what needed doing.

Weeklong sesshins were held once a month. After most of these sesshins, some of the monks were assigned to make a pilgrimage to a nearby leper colony. Many patients in these facilities who had been severely disfigured by leprosy (Hansen's disease) chose to remain in these formerly quarantined facilities. On two occasions, I was invited to join this pilgrimage. Upon arrival the monks and patients would chant together, sit together and share a meal together. It was clear that the patients and staff were very grateful, sincere, deferential and joyous to host our visit. Coming from a weeklong sesshin and then attending at a leper colony made a significant impact on me. Here I felt more like a priest than ever before. The genuine, simple act of sharing time with those who had suffered so much melted my heart. I was humbled by the kindness and attentiveness of everyone participating in this gathering, and I will never forget the deep joy of service and respect offered freely to our fellow beings. We are after all one family of earthlings, none of us are islands, and we are not only inseparable, but also indisputably interdependent.

Every November Ryutaku-Ji becomes a show place for the many hanging scrolls stored there of the art and calligraphy of Zen Masters Hakuin Ekaku (1686 –1769) and his chief disciple Torei Enji (1721 – 1792). Life size effigies, including death masks of these two founding abbots, are on permanent display in the founder's room. People from around the country descend on the temple to have a chance to walk among these masterpieces. All the monks at the temple were expected to sit in meditation as silent guardians while visitors quietly moved from artwork to artwork. During brief breaks I too could marvel at the subtle, profound brush strokes of *sumi* (hand-ground black ink) on paper. One vision that stands out to me was a horse head painted by Hakuin; with a few strokes of his brush, the vivid, vibrant essence of the horse's head was fully revealed. I never tire of looking at this kind of art, and I know now that one's life cannot be full unless there is some place for our creative flow to manifest in our lives.

Between sesshins, most of every day was spent cleaning inside the temple in the mornings, and outside the temple during the afternoons, mainly sweeping the many paths on the temple grounds. We were expected to do all this endless work silently and peaceably. Once I was caught whistling while I swept the grounds with a handmade bamboo broom and was scolded, "*Damei!*" (no good, not serving its purpose; useless). I heard this exclamation a lot during my time at Ryutaku-Ji and so did all the other junior monks. After I got a painful crack in the callus on the ball of my foot from walking barefoot on the below-freezing wooden temple floors, someone noticed that I was limping while dusting in the temple and again I was told, "*Damei!*", implying that I was not to show that I was in pain. Soon I learned to better ignore my own likes and dislikes and just do what needed doing with as little fuss or objection as possible. Over time, I began to deeply appreciate the simplicity, efficiency and mindfulness cultivated by repetitively doing the same chores day after day.

RETURNING TO SEATTLE

Early in January 1982 the temple got a call saying I would need to return home a month early because of a family emergency. Shortly after returning, I began training again with the SZC, and leading introductory zazen once a week. At that time, I was also regularly attending University Friends Meeting (UFM) and in 1983 petitioned to become a member of the Society of Friends. The Quakers examining my membership application asked me many questions about how I could be both a Zen Buddhist and a Quaker. I responded that for me the tree of the Buddhist faith and the tree of the Christian faith were two entirely different species of trees, but that after all they were both trees, drawing from the same water table and reaching for the same light. I also explained that, in my view, even though these two great trees stood apart from each other on opposite banks of the great river of the divine flow of the universe, there were branches of these trees that reached across the divide and gently mingled. The intersections of these branches are for me the Zen and Quaker methods of practice. I showed up at the Meeting House for worship on Sundays, then, as I do now, in my Zen robes with my *zafu* (meditation cushion) and sat cross-legged on the floor. When asked how I can walk both these paths at once, I said, "I walk just fine with two legs, one Buddhist, the other Christian." The Quakers accepted my membership, and I continue to walk easily with both faith traditions. Sunday's silent worship at UFM feels like a diamond in the rough, big, not very polished, yet is the basis for excellent social justice work in the wider world. The Zen diamond by comparison is small but very polished. In my opinion, the Zen tradition needs to recover more of its potential for compassionate action in the wider world. In other words, these two faith traditions can learn a lot from each other.

I remember well studying the words of Jesus in Quaker Bible study, led by Irna Marshall, using the book: *Records of the Life of Jesus.* Irna Marshall was a short, squat, nearly blind, Quaker elder with a bit of a prickly personality and a very warm heart. Her approach to examining the life of Jesus reminded me a lot of how the Zen Masters I came to know approached Buddhist lore and Zen stories. Quaker Bible study consisted of reading a passage from one of the four gospels and working to understand each encounter with Jesus from every perspective. What did Jesus mean when he said what he said? Where was the disciple, questioner, Pharisee or Roman coming from? Each line and encounter were treated as a Zen koan. In this way all of us studying together were looking for new insights into old stories.

Irna dropped her body many years ago, but she will always be in my heart, and remains an inner teacher of mine.

FOUNDING OF CHOBO-JI AND MEETING CAROLYN STEVENS

Over time, tensions around teaching style built up between Glenn Webb and Genki Takabayashi. Eventually, it became clear to me that a separation was likely. In early spring of 1984 Genki told me he no longer could work with Glenn and proposed that we form a temple directly around his teaching style. I was in the group that followed Genki, which he formalized around the temple name, Daibai-zan Chobozen-Ji or more simply, Chobo-Ji (Listening to the Dharma Zen Temple). We had an opening ceremony on September 10, 1984 in the rented house where Genki was living. The group that followed Glenn set up their own residential practice in a house that they rented north of the University of Washington campus. The Seattle Zen Center continued to function under Glenn's guidance until 1986, when he accepted an offer to head up the Fine Arts Division at Pepperdine University in Malibu. After Glenn's departure the Seattle Zen Center faded away. Glenn and I remain in contact with each other and often exchange writings.

I see both Glenn and Genki as two of my core teachers. In mid-1982, I attended a war tax resistance counseling workshop facilitated by Irwin Hogenauer and hosted by Carolyn Stevens, a fellow UFM member. Irwin was born in 1912 and raised in the Bronx, New York. He was involved in peace work from the early 1930's forward as a conscientious objector, non-violent civil disobedience activist, community organizer, and counselor to tax resisters. He spent two years at McNeil Island Penitentiary in Washington State because he would not serve in WWII. During the late 1960s he was a radio anti-war commentator. I felt fortunate and honored to be taught and mentored by him. It was from Rev. Daizen Victoria, Fr. Greg Galluzzo, Archbishop Raymond Hunthausen, Irwin Hogenauer and Carolyn Stevens that I learned how to be a spiritually based activist. Unfortunately, I did not have much time with Irwin as he died late in 1984; my family remained close to his wife, Betty Hogenauer, until her death in 2003. Betty was like a surrogate grandparent to me.

By the time my daughter Adrienne was two years old, my relationship with Diane, my partner since 1980, had seriously deteriorated on many levels, including lack of intimacy. Meanwhile, Carolyn Stevens and I were traveling all around Washington, Oregon and Montana giving War Tax Resistance workshops, becoming deep friends. During our trip to Montana in 1985 we stopped at my aunt's place in Hamilton and she asked me privately if there was something "going on" between us. I assured her that nothing was "going on." However, with my relationship to Diane in deep trouble, I certainly was vulnerable to the attraction I was indeed feeling towards Carolyn. In short, over the next couple of years my relationship with Diane continued to deteriorate and my relationship with Carolyn deepened. The dissolution of my partnership with Diane was one of the hardest trials of my life.

Carolyn and I were married and held a Ceremony for Commitment at University Friends Meeting on September 7, 1991. After numerous ups and downs Carolyn and I remain very much in love and committed to each other. With Diane and her partner, we all co-parented my daughter Adrienne. We are loving friends with Carolyn's former partner and family, and through them we met Fr. William (Bix) Bichsel, S.J., a deep spiritual companion and mentor for both of us. Bix was born in Tacoma, Washington in 1928 and ordained as a Jesuit priest in 1959. At one point he was assigned to the St. Leo Parish in the Hilltop neighborhood of Tacoma, Washington, and there helped establish the Tacoma Catholic Worker community. Bix practiced a life of community organizing, peacemaking and civil resistance. I went on many protest marches with him and once got arrested with him at the Trident Submarine base in Bangor, Washington when we tried to meet with the base commander about the need for nuclear disarmament. It was one of the proudest moments of my life to get arrested with him. He was 86 when he died in 2015. There is no doubt in my mind that he was a living Bodhisattva (Buddhist term for a saint that gives their all for others). He will live on in the hearts and minds of many.

No one can give us a breakthrough, no one can teach us enlightenment; on the other hand, without good modeling and support our natural ability for spiritual awakening is greatly diminished and abiding maturity impossible. Long-term, stable, trusting, non-abusive relationships are essential to our healthy development. I have been exceedingly fortunate to have long-term mentors, spiritual companions and a wonderful partner who meet and exceed these qualifications. Of course, mistakes will be made in every relationship, but in healthy, trusting relationships with good communication skills, these mistakes are more easily negotiated and learned from. To stay together after a breach of trust requires skillful means to process and heal the breach without relying on blame (right-and-wrong thinking) and a willingness with faith to offer renewed trust. This is only possible with complete transparency, honesty, and offering what amends can be made, without requiring a pound of flesh. I hope most of us have discovered that being in deep love with another is a whole lot like being seamless with the Divine. In a healthy relationship both remain individuated, but on another level, there is complete union. When the artificial barriers begin to drop between self and other, we become aware of a mystical union, sharing a common heart-mind.

A JOURNEY WITH JOSHU SASAKI

Joshu Sasaki, considered the elder statesman of Rinzai Zen in the United States, was the founder of the Mt. Baldy Zen Center near Los Angeles. He was born in 1907, came from Japan to teach in the West in 1962 and died in 2014 at the age of 107. Genki began doing sesshins with him in Los Angeles, New Mexico, Cuba and Spain. Soon some of Genki's students, including me, began to follow Genki's lead, joining him for sesshins at Sasaki's temple in New Mexico, Bodhi Manda, in the mid 1980's. I think I went to three sesshins with him there, and Joshu Sasaki came to one sesshin in Seattle (in 1986, I think). Joshu wanted Genki to move to L.A. to take over Rinzai-Ji, Joshu's Zen center in East L.A., and for some time Genki strongly considered this move. Genki even asked me if I would move with him. Frankly, neither Genki nor I were excited by the prospect of leaving Seattle, but we were by this time both smitten with the clarity and charisma of Joshu Sasaki.

During one of my early dokusans with Joshu, I presented a response to a koan that I had read in a book about koans of this type. Joshu immediately tossed me out, telling me never to read such books, because they have the effect of diluting and corrupting one's own insight. In every dokusan that I had with him, I had the feeling he knew exactly where I was at and saw right through me. From that point forward, I never based my responses on anything other than my own direct experience. It was a good lesson.

At the one sesshin Joshu Sasaki attended in Seattle, I served as Genki's English interpreter when he gave instruction and Dharma talks. Genki spoke in *Chobo-go*, the pidgin language of Japanese-English we had developed together, and I translated Chobo-go into colloquial English. To Joshu Sasaki's ear Chobo-go sounded like stilted Japanese with a little English thrown in. When he heard me translate a Dharma talk for Genki, he then asked me if I would translate for him! I told him that I didn't speak Japanese and he had a hard time believing me! I have a favorite picture from the conclusion of that sesshin with my three-year-old daughter sitting in his lap surrounded by all the sesshin participants.

After the conclusion of the last sesshin I attended with Sasaki at Bodhi Manda, I remember being in a private conversation with a monk of his. We were both telling each other stories about our relationships to our Zen Masters. I related the troubles we had had with Genki making overtures to female students that were not always rejected. Sasaki's monk told me of a woman who had written a poem that she made public about the abusive sexual advances made by Sasaki during dokusan! I was shocked, confused and saddened to learn of this. When, soon after, Genki rejected the idea of moving to East L.A., I was much relieved. The relationship between Genki and Sasaki slowly deteriorated from that point forward, until neither Genki nor other Chobo-Ji Sangha members were attending Sasaki sesshins.

PACIFIC NORTHWEST PROGRAM IN SPIRITUAL DIRECTION

As early as 1977 I began doing prison work helping to teach and support inmates doing meditation. The first prison I visited was the McNeil Island Federal Penitentiary, a short ferry ride across Puget Sound from Tacoma, Washington. At that time, I was a support person for Hirano Osho-san and Glenn Webb. I have since done volunteer prison work at Clallam Bay Correction Center, Washington State Reformatory, Twin Rivers Corrections Center, King County Jail and the Washington State Penitentiary. From 1985 to 1988 I served as the principal Buddhist Representative at the Twin Rivers Corrections Center, driving out once a week to lead meditation. Today I continue to visit the Washington State Penitentiary in Walla Walla once a year to lead inmates in meditation. Working with the complex psychological issues inmates and members of my own spiritual communities began to raise with me often left me feeling perplexed. About the only thing I could offer as a Zen priest and Quaker was a willingness to listen and the offer to "let's sit together in meditation." Essentially, I was being asked to be a spiritual companion, and I didn't feel particularly qualified for this role. Therefore, I began to search for a program where I could pick up some additional skills. I found the Pacific Northwest Program in Spiritual Direction (today called the Pacific Jubilee Program - PJP), based at the time at the Vancouver School of Theology on the campus of the University of Vancouver. My Quaker Meeting offered a letter of support during the application process for this program. This year and half certificate program was run in Vancouver by Rev. Dr. Donald (Don) Edward Grayston and in Seattle by Rev. John (Jack) P. Gorsuch, both Episcopal priests.

Don was born in Vancouver, BC in 1939. He went to General Theological Seminary in New York and was ordained a priest in 1964. He got his PhD from the Toronto School of Theology where he began his study of Thomas Merton, which he maintained until the end of his life in 2017. In 1985 he founded the Shalom Institute, which focused on the place of peace and justice issues in theological education. From this effort grew the development of the spiritual direction program that I participated in and helped teach for several years. He was deeply concerned about the threat of nuclear weapons and rabid worldwide racism. I last met with him one evening in 2016 when he was visiting Seattle promoting his new book *Thomas Merton and the Noonday Demon*. He wrote in my copy, "To Genjo – The years fall away;

The True Self remains. – Don."

Jack was a native of Denver, born in 1932. He was a graduate of Wesleyan University and Yale Divinity School. He ordained as an Episcopal priest in 1956, and served for 17 years as rector at the Seattle Epiphany Parish, where he spearheaded the effort to permit the ordination of women. In 1975 he was a finalist for Bishop of the Diocese of Olympia. In the early 1980's, Jack and his wife Bev, a psychiatric social worker, brought together their professional skills and experience to teach and write about spiritual life. In 1985 he founded the Center for Spiritual Development at St. Mark's Cathedral in Seattle, which is where I met him. He was a sweet and gentle soul with an easy manner and a loving heart. He wrote a book, *An Invitation to the Spiritual Journey* with a forward by Gerald May. Both Don and Jack died in 2017.

During the spiritual direction program, I met and practiced with three fellow students who became my life-long friends: Tom Cashman, Joseph Cospito and Fred Davis, MD. I am still in regular contact with all three. Tom is a respected colleague in Spiritual Direction. Joseph has become like an older brother. Fred, who is a retired psychoanalyst, became and remains a friend and mentor with whom I consult professionally in my practice as a psychotherapist. Fred has shared with me much of his early traumatic history, a history so brutal that at no time have I ever been exposed to any history that comes close to this level of suffering. Because of this history,

Fred has an uncanny eye for sensing shadow, repression, and denial. I feel very fortunate to be able to consult with him.

Through my association with Jack Gorsuch and the Center for Spiritual Development I met Sister Ellen Stephen, OSH (ES – as everyone who knows her well calls her). She is an Anglican nun in the order of St. Helena, which at that time had a house only a few blocks away from where I was living. For a time, we met regularly and discussed spiritual direction, spiritual formation, and the commonalties and differences in faith and practice of the Buddhist and Christian communities of which we were a part. Eventually we became workshop co-presenters. She lives with her community at her order's mother house in North Augusta, South Carolina, and tells me that she reads my temple's quarterly newsletter, *Plum Mountain News*, from cover to cover each time it arrives by post. She refers to our association in both of her books, *Together and Apart: A Memoir of the Religious Life* and *You Really Want to Know?*

Working with Jack, Don and the Seattle cohort associated with the spiritual direction training program gave us a wonderfully rich reading list. We met regularly to discuss, explore and examine the texts, ourselves and our means of faith and practice. Three of the books we read which influenced me the most were *Stages of Faith* by James Fowler, *Breakthrough: Meister Eckhart's Creation Spirituality in New Translation* and *The Collected Works of St. Teresa of Avila, Volume Two, The Interior Castle.* Together, these books, mentors and peers inspired me to write my final integration paper in the summer of 1989 on spiritual development blending the paths of Zen Buddhism and Christianity. The next chapter should be viewed as an addendum to this book, but is presented here because this is the place in my timeline when it was originally written. It is an updated revision of the integration paper I wrote in 1989. Don Grayston, who was responsible for reviewing the original paper, pressed me more than once with offers to help me publish it. I never took him up on the idea, but if I had, this next chapter is the revised work that I would have submitted.

SPIRITUAL AWAKENING: TRANSCENDING THE TRINITY & TEN ZEN OX PICTURES

Introduction

Every spiritual tradition relates one or more paths to spiritual awakening and maturity. I've investigated most deeply some of the paths offered by Christianity and Buddhism. All faiths relate stories of mystical union. Only through spiritual awakening can the narrow egoist perspective of the self and the world be seen through. Spiritual awakening may come gradually or suddenly. In truth I think it is always both gradual and sudden, like a fruit that slowly ripens on a tree and one day is suddenly fully ripe. Realization of ripeness may dawn on us slowly or it may come suddenly if the ripe fruit falls from the tree with a smack on the ground. Spiritual maturity usually begins only after the fruit is fully ripe and a sprout of new growth begins. As the new growth begins to take hold, root and eventually flower, it provides for all creatures great and small, animate and inanimate. Because the love and charity of spiritual growth is so important to the survival of our species and the interdependence of all beings, it is important to examine road maps to spiritual awakening and maturity. This offering is a blending of two such maps, one related in the *Ten Zen Ox Pictures* and accompanying verses by twelfth century Chinese Zen Master Kuoan Shiyuan, the other put forth by St. Teresa of Avila and found in *The Interior Castle*. The scaffolding of this examination starts with the Ten Zen Ox Pictures, reinforced by Teresa's journey into The Interior Castle, and then decorated with verses from Zen Masters, Meister Eckart, the Desert Fathers and Mothers, and the Bible. By exploring and blending these two maps of spiritual awakening, I hope my enthusiasm and awe for how two sages, from two different cultures, times, genders and religions can and do speak so eloquently of the human spiritual journey, both skillfully using visualizations and metaphors to prod our own investigation.

I've always been passionately interested in where we came from and why we are here. I suspect these questions, or ones like them, are the start of any journey of spiritual discovery. I was baptized Roman Catholic, but grew up mostly unchurched and curious. To further my own exploration of where we originated, I studied science in college (physics, chemistry, biology and psychology), and shortly after college, in order to be with like-minded seekers of the Way, I joined a Zen Center and a Quaker Meeting. I trained briefly at a Zen temple in Japan in 1981-82 and also trained at Zen temples in New Mexico and New York for many years. I completed a Christian spiritual direction certificate program offered by the Pacific Northwest Program in Spiritual Direction (today called the Pacific Jubilee Program) in 1989. This offering is a reworking of the final integration paper I wrote for this program. I became a Zen monk in 1980. I earned a master's degree in clinical psychology from Antioch University, Seattle in 1991. I was installed as the second abbot of the Zen temple, Chobo-Ji, in Seattle in 1999 and in 2008 I was confirmed as a Dharma Heir in my lineage of Zen.

Most of my exploration has come through dedicated Zen practice and therefore I draw more heavily on Zen sources; nevertheless, I was deeply moved during my spiritual direction studies by readings of ancient and modern Christian mystics. I was blessed to make friends with Meister Eckhart, the Desert Fathers and Mothers, Brother Lawrence, Thomas Merton, and of course, most importantly for this offering, St. Teresa of Avila. Furthermore, during this course of study I established some long-term associations with my mentors and peers. In one way or another, all these relationships, alive or long dead, will last the rest of my life. I've had the good fortune to learn so much from them, and I'm looking forward to learning more. I believe we are all too complicated to grow much on our own without healthy mirroring and mentoring. No one can learn or grow for us; on the other hand, we cannot grow without the support of others.

We don't know for certain who first drew the *Ten Zen Ox Pictures*, but some have attributed them to the 11th century Chinese Zen Master Ching-chu (Jp. Seikyo). Kuòān Shīyun, born in 12th Century China (Jp. Kaku-an Shi-en), wrote the accompanying verses first popularized in the West by Paul Reps and Japanese Zen Master Nyogen Senzaki in their book *Zen Flesh, Zen Bones*. The Zen Ox paintings used here were done by Gyokusei Jikkihara (1904-2005) and I first viewed Gyokusei's paintings in the book *The Zen Life*, by Koji Sato. Within the Zen tradition there are many ways of relating spiritual unfolding. Most of them are shorter and, in my view, less complete or inclusive than what is depicted by the *Ten Zen Ox Pictures*. This sequence uses metaphor and poetry to stimulate investigation of the journey of spiritual awakening. For Kuoan's verse and commentary, I've melded two prominent English translations, one found in *Zen Flesh Zen Bones* and the other in *Buddhism and Jungian Psychology* by J. Marvin Spiegelman and Mokusen Miyuki. The Ox in this context is a metaphor for our deep sage nature, which ninth century Chinese Zen Master Linji Yixuan (Jp. Rinzai) said is the true person, beyond rank and post, going in and out of our face all the time, and which the Quakers refer to as the still small voice that is always with us, but not always heard.

St. Teresa of Avila was a Spanish noblewoman who chose a monastic life as a Carmelite nun. She was known as a mystic, religious reformer, author and theologian of the contemplative life. She was canonized forty years after her death in 1622, and proclaimed the first female Doctor of the Church by Pope Paul VI in 1970. She wrote her seminal work, *The Interior Castle*, in 1577 as a guide for spiritual development. It was inspired by her vision of the soul moving ever deeper in relationship to the divine by journeying through an interior castle of seven mansions, each enclosing the other, until at the center of the castle union with God by transcending the Trinity is realized. For the English translation of *The Interior Castle*, I use volume two of *The Collected Works of St. Teresa of Avila*. With enough exploration, spiritual awakening is guaranteed. In fact, spiritual awakening is not all that hard to come by and is certainly not limited to saints and sages. However, let's face it, humans are so inherently complex that we are easily entangled, and these entanglements interfere with our growth. The complexes arising from our wounds can lead to lifelong patterns of corruption. In addition, we all have a very primitive and one might say "crazy core" driven by instincts for survival and managed by our limbic brain. Our complexes and primitive crazy core can strongly interfere with our spiritual unfolding. It is impossible to escape our complexities and primitive core. If these aspects are denied, rejected, unprocessed and unintegrated, we may still have spiritual awakenings, but never have much spiritual maturity.

Have you ever observed yourself being crazy and enlightened at the same time? In 1989, I watched my child go through a bizarre illness that required hospitalization. My daughter was only five at the time. One day she couldn't eat, the next she couldn't walk. Her immune system systematically attacked different nerves in her body, causing various forms of debilitation. On wide areas of her skin we could see concentric circular red patches that looked a lot like targets. It is frightening to be confronted with how fragile and mortal we are. Observing my reaction to her plight was illuminating. I found myself alternating between distracted thoughts of imminent disaster and a deep serenity where I was able to accept things as they were, comforting her in her suffering, and working to support what could be changed or improved. I found myself crazy with fear and dread, while also being calm and strong. We often find that we are at once primitive and sophisticated. We always have access to our instinctual, primitive fight-flight-freeze responses. At the same time, we may have insights and strength that we can actualize as compassionate action.

Facilitating awareness of the real and transcendent is perhaps the primary goal of spiritual counsel and companionship. Throughout the course of my practice, I have had the great honor and privilege to develop and hone my skills as a good listener and spiritual friend. Always, I'm investigating how egocentric or attached I may be to the course of another's spiritual unfolding. Am I able to maintain neutrality and be sensitive and real without clinging to my idea of a good outcome? Are those who come to see me as a priest, spiritual companion or counselor feeling supported or judged, helped or harmed? Do I find the encounters with others useful? Is my own sense of value dependent on this? Am I able to stay out of the way enough for the Holy Spirit/Inner Light/Buddha Nature/True Self of the directee to inform and direct him or her, rather than me? Am I directive enough to constantly point the directee towards the truths underlying beliefs, images, icons, hierarchy and scripture? Do I find myself dependent on the financial support I receive for this work, and is this a problem? There are no black and white answers to these questions. Nevertheless, most of the time I'm confident that I'm maintaining enough distance without sacrificing intimacy or sensitivity. As to the question of ego involvement and attachment, there is undeniably an element of this in whatever I do; however, I feel minimally encumbered by this fact, because long ago I learned not to take responsibility for another's healing or growth. The best I can do is to be a finger pointing at the real and transcendent. Moreover, I learned that anything "great" done by "me" is mostly a figment of my ego's imagination.

I'm more convinced than ever that all relevant revelation and profound insight comes from a common source or ground. In my view, this palpable ground of being is independent of time or place, culture, species, or planet. Perhaps whales or other self-aware creatures on other planets share our insights! Of course, they won't experience them in the same way, given that whale nature and communication is of necessity considerably different than human nature and communication. Nonetheless, I know that there is a perceptible ground to all being, life and consciousness that is not separate from nor dependent on the sum of all material aspects of the universe. I say "I know" because I'm more confident of its existence than I am of my own. My perception of the intimate-infinite-presence feels much more dependable than my own meager physical form and self-awareness. My deep exploration gives me faith that my consciousness and physical form arise from this intimate-infinite-presence, are animated by *it* moment to moment and return to it after death, just as every ocean wave returns to the ocean. On the one hand, each of us is less than a transient speck in the cosmic fabric; on the other hand, each of us is a manifestation of Christ Consciousness or Buddha Nature. Which is to say, yes, we are both a particle and a wave. Beyond these images, we are all becoming, and we are all companions in this perpetually flowering universe. No words can adequately express the feeling of being an integral, inseparable aspect of *This*.

Opening ourselves to the real and transcendent is what the spiritual journey is all about. St. Teresa of Avila implies that the Trinity is a metaphor that dissolves when we transcendently experience what is real and absolute. Anytime we try to name, divide, or codify that which is inherently indivisible, immutable, infinite, and inconceivable, we are at best pointing a finger at the moon, and at worst fooling ourselves and others. Nevertheless, the sages of every time and culture try their best to communicate their path of understanding, wisdom and compassion, by sharing the skills required to realize and manifest our deep inheritance and true potential. It is my hope that by blending the spiritual awakening maps of twelfth century Zen Master Kuoan Shiyuan's and sixteenth century St. Teresa of Avila's, we might recognize that the journey of awakening transcends East and West, gender, time and culture.

Mostly I try to let these two mystics speak for themselves, interspersed with my own commentary and populated with additional quotations from other numinous writers from both the East and West. Remember that a map is never the territory; moreover, deep clarity is also impermanent and may well be followed by a dark night of the soul. Peak experiences and glimpses of beyond the beyond are very real, but are at best only a starting point for deep maturity. Maturity requires repeatedly walking the labyrinth of spiritual awakening in the midst of our personal trials and tribulations and the sufferings of the world.

The Journey begins...

One: Searching for the Ox

*In the pasture of this world, I endlessly push
aside the tall grasses in search of the ox.
Following unnamed rivers, lost upon the
interpenetrating paths of distant mountains,
My strength failing and my vitality exhausted,
I cannot find the ox.
I only hear the cicadas singing through the
forest at night.*

Kuoan's Comment: "The ox never has been lost. What

need is there to search? Only because of separation from my true nature, I fail to find him. In the confusion of the senses, I lose even his tracks. Far from home, I see many crossroads, but which way is the right one I know not. Greed and fear, good and bad, entangle me."

The ox never has been lost. What need is there to search? Only because of separation from my true nature, I fail to find him. Similarly, here is how St. Teresa speaks about entering the first room of the interior castle:

It seems I'm saying something foolish. For if this castle is the soul, clearly one doesn't have to enter it since it is within oneself. How foolish it would seem were we to tell someone to enter a room he is already in. But you must understand that there is a great difference in the ways one may be inside the castle. For there are many souls who... don't care at all about entering the castle, nor do they know what lies within that most precious place, nor who is within... You have already heard in some books on prayer that the soul is advised to enter within itself; well that's the very thing I'm advising. (St. Teresa, p.285, I:1:5)

I'm always amazed but not really surprised that a twelfth century Zen Master and a sixteenth century Catholic saint can share the same intuitive insight. How can we be anything other than who we are? From the beginning of our journey, we learn that for all our longing we can't really move from where we are now. Hence, our spiritual journey is one through a gateless gate to a more profound awareness of the here and now. "Awareness" is the turning-word (key concept). When I am less aware, it is hard not to be mired in dualism and a dire sense of separation. For others, a lack of significant individuation may manifest itself as a fear of being swallowed up or absorbed by Oneness or Sunyata (Emptiness). It is hard not to seek truth and happiness outside of oneself. The remedy is vigilance, faith and determination, reflection and meditation.

In the confusion of the senses, I lose even his tracks. Far from home, I see many crossroads, but which way is the right one I know not. Greed and fear, good and bad, entangle me. Teresa notes that people in the first rooms "are still absorbed in the world and engulfed in their pleasures and vanities, with their honors and pretenses..." (St. Teresa, p. 293, I:2:12) It is not our senses or the world that stand in our way. Our problem is that we are engulfed, entangled and absorbed by our own attachments, fears and judgements. Standing at home, we become so disoriented that we don't know who we are, let alone where we are or how to get back.

The last line of Kuoan's poem reads, "I only hear the cicadas singing through the forest at night." This is the thread to follow for returning or discovering home.

It contains the hint that we can never be really lost. In this line, "only" is the turning-word: if we only would not belittle our own innate talents and the reality right in front of our nose. Oh, that we could realize that to truly "hear" with any of the senses is to be truly present to the here and now and to whom we truly are. Zen meditation students are often told, "just sit, breathe, and listen." Teresa says, "Insofar as I can understand, the door of entry to this castle is prayer and reflection." (St. Teresa, p. 286, I:1:7)

Two: Seeing the Traces

Along the riverbank under the trees,
  I discover footprints!
Even under the fragrant grass I see his prints.
Deep in remote mountains they are found.
These traces no more can be hidden than
  one's nose, looking heavenward.

Kuoan's Comment: "Understanding the teaching, I see the traces of the ox. Then I learn that, just as many utensils are made from one metal, so too are myriad entities made from the fabric of Self. Unless I discriminate, how will I perceive the true from the untrue? Not yet having entered the gate, nevertheless I have discerned the path. Seeing the traces and glimpsing the teaching is hearing the call of God's voice. Who does not recall a time of being struck by the majesty and mystery of a sunset? Or perhaps you heard the call while listening to a beautiful music and were caught by an inner resonance. These kinds of experiences are often the beginning of the inner journey. "Then I learn that, just as many utensils are made from one metal, so too are myriad entities made from the fabric of Self." If the call is strong enough and the encounter deep enough, then we realize that the majesty and mystery we see, hear and feel is a reverberation of an inner depth or reflection of an Inner Light."

"Unless I discriminate, how will I perceive the true from the untrue? Not yet having entered the gate, nevertheless I have discerned the path." We are still confused, mired in judging good and bad, right and wrong, rather than discerning the appropriate compassionate response to the presenting conditions. Teresa says of this stage that "hearing His voice is a greater trial than not hearing it." And, "I say that these rooms involve more effort because those who are in the first dwelling places are like deaf-mutes and thus the difficulty of not speaking is more easily endured by them than it is by those who hear but cannot [yet] speak." (St. Teresa, p. 298, II:1:2)

At this second stage we are both excited and frustrated. If we say anything about our encounter or enthusiasm it seems to always come out wrong, full of wild or vain descriptions, tied up completely with our discriminating mind. The encounter with the ground-of-our-being or God-self is indeed very loveable but oh, so fleeting.

These traces no more can be hidden than one's nose, looking heavenward. Here lies our hope. We must trust that God is no further away than one's nose, that the Ox (inner sage – Christ Consciousness – Buddha Nature) is always ready to accept us if we would just come home. Now is the time for surrender, for getting out of the way, and letting go. It is only by letting go, cutting our attachments to our own preferences, that we can center enough to harmonize once more. Teresa cautions us that "you cannot begin to recollect yourselves by force but only by gentleness..." and advises "that in my opinion it is very important to consult persons with experience; for you will be thinking that you are seriously failing to do some necessary thing. Provided that we don't give up, the Lord will guide everything for our benefit..." (St. Teresa, p. 302-3, II:1:10)

Three: Seeing the Ox

I hear the song of the nightingale.
The sun is warm, the wind is mild, willows
are green along the bank,
Here no one can hide!
What artist can reproduce that splendid head,
those majestic horns?

Kuoan's Comment: "When one hears the voice, one can sense its source. As soon as the six senses merge, the gate is entered. Wherever one enters one sees the head of the ox! This unity is like salt in water, like color in dyestuff.

The slightest thing is not apart from self."

When one hears the voice, one can sense its source.
Now the Ox is seen or sensed at its source. This corresponds
to a *kensho*, or sudden awakening experience. This kind
of occurrence shakes us down to our foundation. This
experience, depending on its depth, may be the cause
for conversion or entering a religious order, and may be
referred to as a rapture, purification, rebirth or even the
great death (cutting our attachment to our ego identity).
It is said the "senses merge" because this experience
represents the harmonizing of one's whole being. "One
sees the head of the ox" proclaims how in this condition
we immediately become aware, perhaps for the first time
as adults, of the song or voice of the universe! This unity
is as transparent as salt in water and as inseparable as
color in dye. For a moment or more we are not apart from
God or apart from our deep Buddha Nature. For once, at
once, we are directly and fully aware of our oneness with
the universe and beyond the beyond. For Teresa, we have
now moved to the third room of the interior castle and
a direct experience of "divine majesty." "What shall we
say to those who through perseverance and the mercy of
God have won these battles and have entered the rooms
of the third stage, if not: Blessed is the [person] who fears
[trusts] the Lord?" (St. Teresa, p. 304, III:1:1)

My own first encounter came during my first
sesshin, a weeklong marathon of Zen meditation in the

summer of 1977. What follows is an account that I have written about elsewhere and paraphrase here as it is pertinent to "Seeing the Ox":

On the morning of the third day of trying to sit full-lotus on the floor my legs were in agony; I had visions of sweating blood. There was no way I could run or protect myself from the discomfort. My choice was between escaping or surrendering. My fleeting thought was that if there were any grounds for my faith then this was the opportunity to meet or surrender to the source. During a particularly gruesome sit, I gave up and let go of my attachments to control, strength and safety. In truth, I was prepared to die, the pain was free to consume me. From this moment on, there was no fear, no time, and no thoughts, and tears began to flow. I cannot say the pain diminished, but it did become distant and inconsequential. There was a profound peace of being completely at home.

When the bell rang, signaling the end of the sit (period of silent contemplation), I got up to do walking meditation with the group, as was our custom. During the walk there was an awareness or grace to the motion that I had never felt before. Turning a corner in the meditation hall, my eyes found a view through a window of fog mixing with trees and grass. No words can do justice to the impact this view made. I wanted to shout to my compatriots, "Don't you hear it?! Don't you see it?!" but there was nothing new to hear or see that hadn't already been there all along. Instead, a steady stream of tears flowed down my face, and a profound joy filled my heart. From that moment my life changed; in some unfathomable way I had experienced my death and rebirth. I knew that if there were any way for me to share or assist others in hearing this "sound of silence" this would be the greatest of all gifts I could give.

Much later I reread the words of Jesus on the cross, "My God, my God, why hast thou forsaken me? Into thy hands I commend my spirit" and I was seeing this phrase in a whole new way. Just who is it who uncovered this experience? *What artist can reproduce that splendid head and those majestic horns?* The danger lies in thinking that it is "I" or "me," and an equal danger lies in thinking that it is not.

Four: Catching the Ox

I seize him with a terrific struggle.
His great will and power are ungovernable.
He charges to the high plateau
    far above the cloud-mists,
Or in an impenetrable ravine he stands.

Kuoan's Comment: "He dwelt in the forest a long time, but I caught him today! Infatuation for scenery interferes with his direction. Longing for sweeter grass, he wanders away. His mind still is stubborn and unbridled. If I wish him to submit, I must raise my whip."

I caught him today! Who caught who!? *Infatuation for scenery interferes with his direction. Longing for sweeter grass, he wanders away.* Under the pressures of life, I blame the Ox for wandering away. I am likely to feel a sense of abandonment, or, as Teresa says putting it mildly, "dryness." The longing for sweeter grass refers to humility. Harmony is impossible without humility. Teresa advises, "The Lord will give you understanding... so that out of dryness you may draw humility – and not disquiet, which is what the devil aims after. Be convinced that where humility is truly present God will give a peace and conformity... Test us, Lord – for You know the truth – so that we may know ourselves." (St. Teresa, p. 308, III:1:9) Who then is stubborn and unbridled? After a breakthrough there is the hubris of thinking we are complete, but the truth is that we are far from it. We may get the idea that we can now put things right if God will only change a little or do things our way; in which case, our own mind once again binds us and separates us from the one we love and the fullness of who we are.

If I wish him to submit, I must raise my whip. The whip is one of vigilance, silence, reflection, and determination, and it is not the Ox, but I who must submit. "What it seems to me would be highly beneficial for those who through the goodness of the Lord are in this state... is that they study diligently how to be prompt in obedience. And even if they are not members of a religious order, it would be a great thing for them to have – as do many persons – someone whom they could consult so as not to do their own will in anything. Doing our own will is usually what harms us. And they shouldn't seek another of their own making, ... but seek out someone who is very free from illusion about the things of the world." (St. Teresa, p. 314, III:2:12) About a week after my first breakthrough in 1977, I began to doubt my own experience because the realization was no longer as vivid as it had been. I entered a dark night of consternation and doubt that lasted a little over a year. Towards the end of this time I began to realize I really couldn't know anything for certain. My very identity was in doubt. Who am I if I am not the spiritual being I thought I was? For me to recover required surrendering more completely to my Zen practice and my Zen teacher Genki Takabayashi. Even amid my own Great Doubt, I committed to becoming a Zen monk and was ordained a Zen unsui (novice monk – cloud and water person) in 1980.

Five: Taming the Ox

The whip and the rope are necessary,
Else he might stray off down some dusty road.
Being well trained,
*   he becomes naturally gentle.*
Then, unfettered, he obeys his master.

Kuoan's Comment: "When one thought arises, another thought follows. When the first thought springs from enlightenment, all subsequent thoughts are true. Through delusion, one makes everything untrue. Delusion is not caused by objectivity; it is the result of subjectivity. Hold the nose-ring tight and do not allow vacillation."

This stage corresponds to Teresa's fourth and the start of the fifth level within the interior castle: "Since these dwelling places now are closer to where the King is, their beauty is great." Having conditioned ourselves with humility, trust, faith, diligence and determination, we are ready by the grace of God to experience what Teresa calls "spiritual delights." She says that up to this point God's grace is experienced as primarily limited to consolations that seem to come from afar via aqueducts. Now in the fourth level, God's grace is experienced more constantly and directly like a fountain from a deep spring. (St. Teresa, p. 323-4, IV:2:3-4) Spiritual delights coming from a deep interior spring are exactly what is meant by the line, "When one thought arises, another thought follows. When the first thought springs from enlightenment, all subsequent thoughts are true."

Teresa writes, "How can I explain the riches and treasures and delights found in the fifth dwelling places? I believe it would be better not to say anything about these remaining rooms, for there is no way of knowing how to speak of them; neither is the intellect capable of understanding them nor can comparison to help and explaining them; earthly things are to coarse for such a purpose." (St. Teresa, p. 335, V:1:1) Though, as Teresa attests, "Poisonous creatures rarely enter these dwelling places," there is still a significant danger that we can be distracted enough to start old dusty tapes of self-delusion, and we know that, "Through delusion, one makes everything untrue." Therefore, we must remain diligent to our call to love God with all our heart and mind, and seek only to do the will of the Lord. Our tapes of self-delusion are never created or restarted by any centered (objective) process of discernment. Tapes are created or restarted when we make self-fooling (subjective) responses to difficult circumstances. For children, this is virtually unavoidable; however, by the stage represented by the fifth Zen Ox picture, we are hopefully mature enough to rule circumstances rather than having them rule us. Nevertheless, we must hang on tight, probably with a discipline that allows little room to maneuver on our own, or we may find ourselves alone again down some dusty (self-delusional) road.

One period of my life that roughly corresponds to this phase of unfolding was the time between the spring of 1980 and early 1982. I was ordained in October of 1980 and began my training period in Japan almost exactly a year later. In the early days in Japan circumstances were difficult enough to shake my confidence thoroughly. I found myself feeling more separate and alone than I could ever remember. It was an awful time, but as Teresa predicted some four-hundred years ago, "If they [poisonous creatures] enter they do no harm; rather, they are the occasion of gain." Through perseverance, by the time I left Japan early in 1982 my faith and trust had matured considerably, though of course both would be tried severely many times afterwards.

Six: Riding the Ox Home

Riding the ox, slowly I return homeward.
The voice of my flute intones
through the evening.
Measuring with hand-beats the pulsating
harmony, I direct the endless rhythm.
Whoever hears this melody will join me.

Kuoan's Comment: "The struggle is over; gain and loss are assimilated. I sing the song of the village woodsman, and play the tunes of the children. Astride the Ox, I observe the clouds above. Onward I go, no matter who may wish to call me back."

The sixth picture corresponds roughly to Teresa's fifth, sixth and start of seventh dwelling place. It is in this place that Teresa begins to tell of the rapture of spiritual union. As I explained earlier, the Zen Ox picture model allows for an initial breakthrough in the third picture that corresponds to Teresa's third dwelling place. The difference here is that the sense of communion is so regular as to be commonplace. In other words, in this dwelling place one can rest regularly in the presence of the Inner Light. People at this phase find themselves drifting briefly in and out of spiritual union, without long gaps between encounters. Feeling securely on the path home, our trust and faith are enough to let the Ox lead us; we are content to rest in Jesus' arms and confident that the Lord will be with us while facing any trial. We may be thrown from the Ox's back at any time, but in this phase, unless it is a big fall, it is relatively simple to remount and continue. *Onward I go, no matter who may wish to call me back.* When riding the Ox, there is great peace of mind. It feels for a time that all we need to do is ride and go where the Ox will take us. We regress only when there is a big enough storm of circumstances (sufferings of life) to be knocked hard off the Ox's back. While we are riding the Ox, the whip and tether needed in earlier phase are put aside because during the ride they are sweetly integrated into our being.

The comment "gain and loss are assimilated" means that we no longer make or find our treasure in the world, but lay up our treasures in heaven and God. "Astride the Ox, I observe the clouds above." "I sing the song of the village woodsman, and play the tunes of the children" means that the process of individuation and early integration is feeling complete. In this phase we have full communion with our childlike nature while retaining the discernment of an adult. *Whoever hears this melody will join me.* This line implies that one in this condition no longer needs or desires to overtly proselytize on behalf of their faith-tradition; living one's life becomes the best advertisement. The serenity and song (compassionate ministry) exuding from such a person spontaneously announces the good news that living life in accordance with the Way (Tao – Holy Spirit) is possible.

"There is no need here to use any technique to suspend the mind since all of the faculties are asleep in the state – and truly asleep – to the things of the world and to ourselves... In sum, it is like one who in every respect has died to the world so as to live more completely in God." (St. Teresa, p. 336, V:1:4) "the silk worm, which is fat and ugly, then dies, and a little white butterfly, which is very pretty, comes forth from the cocoon." (St. Teresa, p. 340 V:1:11) "the soul fears nothing and is absolutely determined to overcome every obstacle for God. And the reason is that it is always so closely joined... that from this union comes it's fortitude." (St. Teresa, p. 360, VI:1:2)

Having been knocked off the Ox many times, a few times pretty hard, I no longer have much fear or doubt about getting back on. Make no mistake, from time to time I can be overwhelmed by waves of difficult circumstances, but I always seem to end up on the beach instead of drowning. Testing is an integral part of the spiritual journey, and we will fall or fail and feel isolated from the divine again and again. Teresa describes the union experienced in the fifth and sixth rooms to be "like the joining of two wax candles to such an extent that the flame coming from them is but one, or that the wick, the flame and the wax are all one. But afterward one candle can be easily separated from the other and there are two candles; the same holds for the wick." (St. Teresa, p. 434, VII:2:4) From time to time we are one with the divine, but we are also easily separated from the Other. I believe that Teresa also means to say, from time to time we feel as one with our neighbor, without ever being the same. We are all unique but never separate. Often, I feel one with my spouse and we remain uniquely individuated. Each one of us is a unique wave of the divine, never separate from the whole ocean. When doubt arises, we try to remember that we are two and not two.

Happily, after more than forty years of practice, it feels as though I spend most of my time in this phase of the journey. When riding the Ox becomes second nature, all the rooms or phases are visited regularly and seamlessly, gently settling again and again upon the Ox's back. In this phase, I have a clear idea of self, while hopefully rarely being possessed by an egocentric agenda.

Most of the time it feels easy to allow the Ox (inner sage) to effortlessly and joyously direct this life. "The soul sees is clearly that if it has anything good this is given by God and is by no means its own." (St. Teresa, p. 361, VI:1:4)

Seven: Ox Forgotten, Self Alone

Astride the ox, I reach home.
I am serene. The ox is no more.
The dawn has come. In blissful repose,
Within my thatched dwelling I have
abandoned the whip and rope.

Kuoan's Comment: "All is one law, not two. We only make the ox a temporary subject. It is as the relation of rabbit and trap, of fish and net. It is as gold and dross, or the moon emerging from a cloud. One path of clear light travels on throughout endless time."

The seventh picture corresponds to the full betrothal of the individual to the Trinity. This is represented in Teresa's imagery as a butterfly emerging from its cocoon, which appears at the end of the sixth dwelling place and somewhat overlaps with Teresa's imagery of a spiritual marriage found in the seventh dwelling place. All is one, not two. In this phase we fully realize that the Ox is only a metaphor for our deep nature. In this phase no state of enlightenment is sought. No longer lost in a sea of self-delusions, we find ourselves where we are, where we have always been, at home. It is, as Zen Master Baizhang Huaihai (Jp. Hyakujo Ekai) puts it, like "sitting entirely alone atop a great sublime peak." Paul tells us, "...he that is joined unto the Lord in one spirit." (1Cor. 6:17) When we fully realize that we are one spirit with the Lord, then even the words Ox, Lord, Divine, Buddha, Dharma, become superfluous. Teresa says that a spiritual marriage is "like what we have when rain falls from the sky into a river or fount; all is water, for the rain that fell from heaven cannot be divided or separated from the water of the river. Or it is like what we have when a little stream enters the sea, there is no means of separating the two." (St. Teresa, p. 434, VII:2:4)

Recall or imagine what it is like to realize that we are fully seamless with Christ or Buddha nature. Our ego will feel as a rabbit ensnared in a trap or a fish caught in a net. *It is as gold and dross, or the moon emerging from a cloud.* "God is love; and he that dwelleth in love dwelleth in God, and God in him." (1John 4:16) In this phase, our rebirth or emergence is complete and we are free to be useful, responsible, and unattached to our desires. We are free to manifest our deepest creative potential and free to love to our fullest extent. In this condition, our fear of death is completely transcended. "There is no fear in love; but perfect love casteth out fear: because fear hath torment. He that feareth is not made perfect in Love." (1John 4:18) For a time we are no longer dependent on Christ's example, nor dependent on our faith in the resurrection or eternal life. We are deeply humbled and grateful, but not dependent on miracles, scripture, teachers or sages. We find life oh, so precious and valued, but have no need to cling to it. We are free because we realize we are already seamless with the universe and beyond. The timeless self-essence is reached, "Death is swallowed up in victory. O death, where is thy sting? O grave, where is thy victory?" (1Cor. 15:54 & 55).

Within my thatched dwelling I have abandoned the whip and rope. Whip and tether are not needed because they are completely integrated into our being and are therefore not seen. Zen koans (pithy inquiries which are usually derived from the sayings and doings of ancient Zen masters) that stretch the practitioner in this dimension include: "On what does the Buddha ride?", "How does the Buddha walk?", "Demonstrate how Mind is Buddha."

It would be foolish to think that this phase is outside the reach of one's direct personal experience; the same is true of all the Zen Ox Pictures. It is also important to remember that these pictures do not represent fixed sequential steps. All of us from time to time visit most of these pictures. Anyone on a lifelong spiritual journey will certainly stretch in the readiness of time into the states represented by any of the last four pictures. And anytime we access one of these later pictures, a natural and inevitable degradation period sets in. What remains from visiting these latter phases is a measure of new confidence about the breadth of spiritual awakening and some useful insight or even a sense of penetrating clarity into the nature of reality. These excursions happen more frequently as the practitioner becomes more skillful at exploring spiritual depths. The first time we visit the Grand Canyon we are likely to be over-awed by the experience. As we visit more often, the innumerable canyons become more familiar, even ordinary. At the same time, we realize that no matter how often we visit, we will never be able to fully investigate all the canyons of spiritual awakening.

Even if a practitioner becomes skillful enough to regularly visit these latter stages, this alone in no way guarantees maturity. Great explorers, artists, or scientists are not necessarily mature human beings. All Zen masters and sages of any tradition are undoubtedly familiar with all these latter stages, and those serving as spiritual guides to others often rest or dwell in this phase while teaching.

Eight: Both Ox and Self Forgotten

Whip, rope, person, and ox -
all merge in No-Thing.
This heaven is so vast no message can stain it.
How may a snowflake exist in a raging fire?
Here are the footprints of the ancient masters.

Kuoan's Comment: "Mediocrity is gone. Mind is clear of limitation. I seek no state of enlightenment. Neither do I remain where no enlightenment exists. Since I linger in neither condition, eyes cannot see me. If hundreds of birds strew my path with flowers, such praise would be meaningless."

Whip, rope, person, and ox - all merge in No-Thing.

In order that nothing may remain hidden from me in God that has not been revealed, no likeness and no image may remain open in me, for an image does not open up to us either the Godhead or the essence of God. (*Breakthrough: Meister Eckhart's Creation Spirituality* in New Translation, Matthew Fox, p. 126-127)

This heaven is so vast no message can stain it.

Understand now that there is a power in the soul that is wider than the widest heaven, which is so unbelievably wide that we cannot correctly express it. Yet that power is even wider still.... Yesterday I sat in a dwelling place and made a statement that sounded quite unbelievable. I said that Jerusalem is as close to my soul as the place in which I am now. Yes, quite truly, an object a thousand miles farther away than Jerusalem is as near to my soul as is my own body -- and I am as certain of this as I am of the fact that I am a human being. (Eckhart, p. 126-127)

In this phase there is no one to seek enlightenment. When one is blown away without a trace, there is no seeker and no one and nothing to be found but No-Thing (which Eckhart calls Godhead). This picture signifies merging experientially with that which precedes Alpha and Omega, and with that which is the prelude to the Word. In Zen this state is sometimes referred to as "the black before black." Does this sound impossible? The mystics tell us it's not. Unfortunately, many people who never feel the need or call to start the spiritual journey will remain glued to the limited scope of our discriminating mind, which labels everything as this or that and always separates self from other. When the discriminating mind encounters something that is inconceivable, it tends to exclude it from the realm of our perception, or creates a mythology to explain the unknowable. As valuable and ingenious as our discriminating mind is, it is far from our whole mind, which ultimately is boundless. Even though our discriminating mind only represents a fraction of our potential, it normally exhibits such dominance that we usually fail to see beyond its perspective. Only by letting go of the reins of the discriminating, naming, seeking, finding, fixing, analyzing, judging mind, can we hope to find full illumination beyond our limited egoistic perspective.

In the Zen tradition we learn that when it comes to the big questions such as "What is This reality?" and "Who's asking?" and "What is the meaning of life?" there is fundamentally no way of knowing. Knowing is considered a delusion of the rational discriminating mind. However, investigating these very questions is essential and indispensable in facing this Great Matter of Life and Death.

Neither do I remain where no enlightenment exists. Since I linger in neither condition, eyes cannot see me. Most of us go about in a constant state of looking for something that we think we've lost. If it's not our car keys then it's Jesus. "It's a good thing my head is screwed on, otherwise I would have misplaced it" is an apt adage for what we surely have all experienced multiple times. People who are lost are easy to spot, those who are found tend to blend in. Have you noticed that when we meet someone who has found their way that they seem to be inexplicably unconcerned about perfection? Lingering neither in enlightenment or its absence, there is nothing to attain and no perfection found or needed.

If hundreds of birds strew my path with flowers, such praise would be meaningless. Beware of the holier-than-thou false prophets in sheep's clothing. Jesus is recorded in the seventh chapter of St. Matthew as having said, "Ye shall know them by their fruits," yet this chapter starts out with the call to "Judge not..." The desert Father Abba John once said, "the saints are like a group of trees, each bearing different fruit, but watered from the same source. The practices of one saint differ from those of another, but it is the same Spirit that works in all of them." (*The Sayings of the Desert Fathers* [and Mothers], Benedicta Ward, p. 95) All of us have the capacity to bear fruit of one kind or another. A tree must be well nurtured to bear a fruit. It is not our job to feed everyone, it is our job to bear what fruit we can. This is only possible with adequate self-care. It is best to try to give everyone the benefit of the doubt. Most people mean well, and are not trying to fool us for their own gain. On the other hand, it is only prudent to be as aware and discerning as possible. We must constantly ask ourselves, what is appropriate at this time and how shall I act on it? Certainly, a sage does what needs doing without need for praise or attachment to a particular outcome. Praise and scorn are always meaningless to anyone aware of just how deep their roots go.

"The Great Way is not difficult for those unchained to their preferences. When idealization and vilification are both absent, everything becomes clear and undisguised... When the mind exists undisturbed in the Way, nothing in the world can offend, and when a thing can no longer offend, it ceases to exist in the old way. When no discriminating thoughts arise, the old mind ceases to exist." (Sosan Ganchi Verses on the Faith Mind, p.33, Chobo-Ji Sutra Book translation)

"I have said before that one is a poor person who does not even will to fulfil God's will, that is who so lives that he or she is empty both of his own will and of God's will, just as they were when they were not yet. About this poverty we say that it is the highest poverty." (Eckhart, p.216)

The eighth picture represents the heart of what Teresa calls a spiritual marriage in the seventh dwelling place. It is the source of the fountain of interior joy and eternal trust of which Teresa often speaks. Koans used to help meet reality's source include: "What did your face look like before your great-grandparents were born?" "How do you remove a treasure from the bottom of an ocean while sitting on the shore?" Melding with the root of our own being, which is none other than the root of the universe, one is completely gone with no trace remaining, in one step crossing an ocean; returning, one is reborn with a new song in one's heart.

As wonderous as the spiritual marriage may feel, it is not practical to live in this phase. In the Zen tradition, after experiencing one form of enlightenment or another, we are instructed to throw away our enlightenment and just be ordinary. To dwell in enlightenment is another form of distraction. In this phase and the next there is no sense of self and without a sense of self it is impossible to be of service to our troubled world.

Nine: Returning to the source

Too many steps have been taken returning to the root and the source.
Far better is it to stay at home, blind and deaf, and without much ado;
Dwelling in one's true abode, unconcerned with that without--
The river flows tranquilly on and the flowers are red.

Kuoan's Comment: "From the beginning, truth is clear. Poised in silence, I observe the forms of integration and disintegration. One who is not attached to "form" need not be "reformed." The

105

water is emerald, the mountain is indigo, and I see that which is creating and that which is destroying."

From the beginning, truth is clear. What animates us at our foundation? We might call it the Holy Spirit, Buddha Nature, or Inner Light. Can we ever be separated from what enlivens us? Clearly, unless we can figure out a way to take reality out of reality, the answer is no. Of course, we may be estranged from conscious awareness of our connection but we are never abandoned or apart. This Ox picture shows nature as it is, and represents the experiential union with that which animates the cosmos. It is as if we were to meet the Holy Spirit face to face and merge or open our awareness completely; two become one, and we are experientially no more or less than the cosmos as it is. It is all out, everything is revealed, nothing is hidden, and there is no need or even ability to hold on to a separate "self."

Poised in silence, I observe the forms of integration and disintegration. When people encounter this experience, they often report hearing the "Sound of Silence" or tell of being completely gone but not lost. "Integration and disintegration" refer to the cycles and sufferings of birth and death, the seasons and motions of all form. The entire universe is in flux and transitory. When we experience union with this aspect of the Trinity, it is perceived as existential abandon rather than abandonment! "One who is not attached to 'form' need not be 'reformed'." This implies that we become one with all coming and going, which is to say unattached to permanence, and in doing so we find ourselves able to meet any set of circumstances and not be weighed down. We flow with the flow.

The water is emerald, the mountain is indigo, and I see that which is creating and that which is destroying. Alive in alive-ness we know the power of green, of wind and mountain. Being transparent ourselves, we can freely visit with our raven, fox and bear cousins; we are able to befriend the spring flowers, summer wind, autumn moon and winter snow. Koans that poke at this condition are: "Bring me a mountain top in a summer rain." "Tie a rope around the closest mountain and bring it here."

Each of the last three pictures, concluding with this one, represents dwelling places in the seventh room of Teresa's interior castle. To truly reach union with any one of the aspects represented by these pictures is to be unified with all three. It is as though we are standing in one room looking out three different open windows, each with a different view of the world around us. Teresa refers to this unification as a spiritual marriage to the Trinity.

"In this seventh dwelling place the union comes about in a different way: our God now desires to remove the scales from the soul's eyes and let it see and understand, although in a strange way, something of the favor He grants it. When the soul is brought into that dwelling place, the Most Blessed Trinity, all three

Persons, through an intellectual vision, is revealed to it through a certain representation of the truth. First there comes an enkindling in the spirit in the manner of a cloud of magnificent splendor; and these Persons are distinct, and through an admirable knowledge the soul understands as a most profound truth that all three persons are one substance and one power and one knowledge and one God alone. It knows in such a way that what we hold by faith, it understands, we can say through sight -- although the sight is not with the bodily eyes nor with the eyes of the soul, because we are not dealing with an imaginative vision. Here all three Persons communicate themselves to it, speak to it, and explain those words of the Lord in the Gospel: that He and the Father and the Holy Spirit will come to dwell with the soul that loves Him and keeps His commandments." (St. Teresa, p. 430, VII:1:6)

As we shall see in the tenth Ox picture, spiritual marriage completely changes one's life and a new character is born.

Ten: Entering the Marketplace with Helping Hands

Barefooted and naked of breast, I mingle with the people of the world.

My clothes are ragged and dust-laden, and I am ever blissful.

I use no magic to extend my life;

Now, before me, the dead trees become alive.

Kuoan's Comment: "Inside my gate, a thousand sages do not know me. The beauty of my garden is invisible. Why should one search for the footprints of the ancient masters? I go to the market place with my gourd and return home with

109

my staff. I visit the wine shop and the market, and everyone I look upon becomes enlightened. Only after a lifetime of practice can we hope to mature enough to live the character represented by this picture most of the time. During deep realization, brought on by repeated transcendent experiences of reality, every aspect of the Trinity is met and assimilated. In this state, all conceptualizations are seen through and dualistic thinking is relegated to maneuvering in the world. In this condition there is no dependence on rank, post, position, wealth, territory, hierarchy, doctrine, images or icons. When we can enter the complexities of the marketplace with love and equanimity, life and death are no longer a burden or a trial. No hindrance is found in participating fully in life or preparing fully for death, and all activity is recognized as spiritual practice. St. Teresa of Avila lived a life of service; a life of service is entering the marketplace with helping hands."

Abba Matoes said, "He who dwells with brethren must not be square, but round, so as to turn himself towards all." He went on, "It is not through virtue that I live in solitude, but through weakness; those who live in the midst of men are the strong ones." (*Desert Fathers*, p. 145)

Even briefly transcending the Trinity through

direct interior union, one can't help but realize our full human potential, with all the limitations and splendor this implies. Moreover, we also glimpse how we are and have always been much more than this! When we are fully aware of reality as it is, a seamless, infinite, intimate, multi-dimensional, ungraspable reality that is not bounded by doctrine or conceptualizations, then we are at least temporarily free from our egoistic, life-centric, human-dominated view of the world. In Zen this is referred to as satori (deep abiding enlightenment).

"The more people are free of all things and turn to themselves, the more they will know in themselves all things clearly with their reason [consciousness], without any hindrance from outside. And the more they do this, the more they are truly human." (Eckhart, p.168)

We normally perceive creation as full of dualities: self and other, yin and yang, male and female, No-Thing and everything, the Law of cause and effect (relativity) and the Law of uncertainty (quantum mechanics), to name a few. We must remember that discriminating understanding will always be hopelessly limited and often confused, but our deep insight has been and will be unhindered by dualistic thinking, because fundamentally we are seamless with the boundless truth we hope to penetrate. We are living, conscious, self-conscious and

111

completely inseparable aspects of reality. If we can see beyond our surface idea of self, then by extension, we will be seeing beyond our surface perception of reality. There is nothing wrong with the discriminating or scientific mind, it is surely an important and prominent human capacity, but as the mystics throughout time have pointed out, there are other avenues of awareness that can be tapped with skillful means.

"If you wish to move in the One Way do not dislike even the world of senses and ideas. Indeed, to accept them fully is identical with true Enlightenment. ... [Yet,] to seek Mind [full awareness] with the discriminating mind is the greatest of all mistakes. ... just simply say when doubt arises, "Not two." In this "not two" nothing is separate, nothing is excluded. No matter when or where, enlightenment means entering this truth. And this truth is beyond extension or diminution in time or space; in it a single thought is ten thousand years." (Sosan Ganchi, p.35, Chobo-Ji Sutra Book)

Conclusions

Having completed the journey and visited all the Zen Ox pictures and all the rooms in the Interior Castle we realize that Mind is and is not; the Trinity is and is not; time is and is not; motion is and is not; rest is and is not; suffering is and is not; the last shall be first and the first shall be last; you must lose your life in order to find it. Hard to fathom? The third Chinese Zen ancestor in the seventh century tried to give us a hand when he said:

"To deny the existence of things is to miss their reality; to assert the emptiness of things is to miss their reality. The more you talk and think about it, the further astray you wander from the truth. Stop talking and thinking, and there is nothing you will not be able to know. To return to the root is to find the meaning, but to pursue appearances is to miss the source. At the moment of inner enlightenment there is a going beyond appearance and emptiness. The changes that appear to occur in the empty world we call real only because of our ignorance. Do not search for the truth; only cease to cherish opinions.

Do not remain in the dualistic state; avoid such pursuits carefully. If there is even a trace of this and that, of right and wrong, the Mind-essence will be lost in confusion. Although all dualities come from the One, do not be attached even to this One. When the mind exists undisturbed in the Way, nothing in the world can offend, and when a thing can no longer offend, it ceases to exist in the old way." (Sosan Ganchi, p.34)

The person experiencing what the tenth Zen Ox picture is pointing at goes beyond relying on assertion or denial, and black-and-white thinking. Sosan Ganchi says, "If you wish to see the truth then hold no opinions for or against anything. To set up what you like against what you dislike is the disease of the mind. When the deep meaning of things is not understood the mind's, essential peace is disturbed to no avail." Even to say, "God is good" is to go too far, or not far enough.

"If I were to say that God is good, I would be wrong; it is more correct to say that I am good and God is not good. The point I am making is...whatever is good can become better and what is better can become best... all three of these terms -- good, better and best -- are far from God's reality, for he is exalted above everything." (Eckhart, p. 178)

"To whom then will ye liken God? or what likeness will ye compare unto him?" (Is. 40:18)

"If any kind of image or likeness were to remain within you, you would never become one with God.

Therefore, in order that you may become one with God, no image should be represented in you, either inwardly or outwardly. This means that nothing should be concealed in you that does not become unconcealed and tossed away." (Eckhart, p.328)

If all conceptualizations of God fall short, and we realize that our different images of God keep us apart, then why talk about God at all? If we accept that on some level all aspects of the universe are aspects of God, then we cannot speak adequately about the true nature of anything. It is best to give up judging anyone or anything too harshly. All aspects of God are doing the best they can to flow and flower. When deeply deprived and abused we can't help but be primitive, raw and reduced to fight, flight or freeze. On the other hand, when we are not convoluted and our heart-minds are open, it is easy to discern what is appropriate, loving action. This is exactly where we find those who are residing in the tenth Zen Ox picture.

"Obey the nature of things (your own nature), and you will walk freely and undisturbed. When thought is binding the truth is hidden, for everything is murky and unclear, and the burdensome practice of judging brings annoyance and weariness. What benefit can be derived from distinctions and separations?" (Sosan Ganchi, p.35)

No matter how eloquent we are we cannot share truth with another. Transmission can only come about when the one we are trying to communicate with directly experiences the truth for themselves. The best we can do is point our friends in the direction of our own practice and experience. To encourage the development of an open, flexible, heart-mind we need only demonstrate this capacity (compassion, long-suffering, tolerance) ourselves.

"For the Lord gives the soul great stability and good resolutions not to deviate from His service in anything." (St. Teresa, p.444, VII:4:2)

"...you need not be desiring to benefit the whole world but must concentrate on those who are in your company, and thus your deed will be greater since you are more obliged toward them. Do you think such deep humility, your mortification, service of all and great charity toward them and love of the Lord is of little benefit? This fire of love in you enkindles their souls, and with every other virtue you will be always awakening them. Such service will not be small but very great and very pleasing to the Lord." (St. Teresa, p.449-450, VII:4:14)

As children we are dependent because we have not yet developed the skills to live life independently.

Even though every parent is doing the best they can, it is more than likely that our innate freedom, creativity, wisdom, integrity, worthiness are squashed many times during our upbringing. Naturally, we react with anger and fear and end up developing numerous immature coping mechanisms to temporarily pacify our needs. The remnants of these mechanisms become our adult attachments and delusions. When fear is banished via direct transcendent experience of what is real, then attachments and delusions lose their power and meaning. As the veil of fear and its companion, the ignorance of holding on to opinions for or against ourselves or others as truth, lifts, a rebirth takes place, and we are born again as adult children of God.

"When I come to the point when I no longer project myself into any image and fancy no images in myself, and toss away everything within me, then I can be transported into God's naked being, and this is the pure essence of the Spirit. There every comparison must be driven out, so that I can be transported into God and can become one with him and one substance and one essence and one nature and in this way a child of God. And after this has happened, nothing more in God is hidden that will not be revealed or will not be mine." (Eckhart, p.328)

"To fathom the mystery of this One-essence is to be

released from all entanglements. When all things are seen equally the timeless Mind-essence is reached. No comparisons or analogies are possible in this causeless, relationless state. Consider movement stationary and the stationary in motion, both movement and rest disappear. When such dualities cease to exist, Oneness itself cannot exist. To this ultimate finality no law or description applies." (Sosan Ganchi, p.36)

As young adults we leave our parent's home, but we bring a substitute set of parents with us. Our surrogate parents are our idealizations, beliefs and judgments. To become fully adult, we must leave these surrogate parents behind. This thought is both radical and scary.

"Think not that I am come to send peace on earth: I come not to send peace, but a sword. For I am come to set a man at variance against his father, and the daughter against her mother... And a man's foes shall be they of his own household. He that loveth father or mother more than me is not worthy of me." (Matt. 10:34-37)

To live this principle means that we must lose our attachment to our constructed "sense of self." "For whosoever will save his life shall lose it: and whosoever will lose his life for my sake shall find it." (Matt. 16:25) We must find enough faith and trust to let go and let be.

"The Great Way is calm and open hearted. Those who travel it find it neither easy nor difficult, but those with limited views are fearful and irresolute, the faster they hurry, the slower they go, and clinging (attachment) cannot be limited. Even to be attached to the idea of enlightenment is to go astray. Just let things be in their own way and there will be neither coming nor going." (Sosan Ganchi, p.35)

"I emphatically state that, so long as you accomplish your deeds for heaven's sake or God's sake or your eternal happiness from the outside, you are not doing things properly for yourself. You may be accepted, but this is not the best arrangement.... For whoever seeks God in a definite mode [belief system] accepts the mode and misses God, who is hidden in that mode. Whoever seeks God without a mode, however, grasps him as He is in himself." (Eckhart, p. 201)

Eckhart advises: "...let your own 'being you' sink into and flow away into God's 'being God.' Then your 'you' and God's, 'his,' will become so completely one 'my' that you will eternally know with him his changeless existence and his nameless nothingness." (Eckhart, p.179) Teresa tells us that the first effect of a spiritual marriage is "a forgetfulness of self, for truly the soul seemingly, no longer is." (St. Teresa, p.438, VII:3:2)

When we breach the artificial barriers between self and other, we are bound to feel a deep sense of serenity and freedom, which Eckhart refers to as, repose.

"If I were asked to give valid information concerning what the Creator's aims were when he created all creatures, I would say: "Repose."… I love the thing in which I most recognize God's likeness. But nothing resembles God in all creatures so much as repose." (Eckhart, p.380-381)

With repose and not holding too closely our own opinions or those of others, we are free to know what we want and go for it.

"A brother went to see Abba Poemen and said to him, "What ought I to do?" The old man said to him, "Go and join one who says 'What do I want?' and you will have peace." (*Desert Fathers*, p. 187)

"If anyone were to ask… "Why are you alive?" the only reply could be: "I live so that I may live." This happens because life lives without a reason so that it lives for itself. Whoever asked a truthful person who accomplishes deeds from his or her own foundation, "Why do you accomplish deeds?" that person, if he or she were to reply correctly, would say only: "I accomplish so that I can accomplish." (Eckhart, p. 201)

What we want is to accomplish our part as it presents itself. When we are awake our part will be self-sufficient and wholly satisfying without dependence on an outcome. At any given moment our part might be to make amends, plan a future event, or simply do what is in front of us to do. In Zen we say, when hungry prepare a meal, when tired go to sleep, when there is a need, lend a helping hand. The enlightened life is the ordinary life. Being children of God what we want is peace for all; to love our neighbors as ourselves. However, peace does not imply the absence of suffering. Peace of mind grants us the ability to have serenity while suffering or celebrating. Freedom does not imply freedom from suffering; it implies freedom to suffer or not with equanimity. After a deep breakthrough, at least for a short time, we can meet any circumstances, whether good or bad, to our liking or not, with equanimity.

Teresa tells us a great capacity for suffering is one of the effects of a spiritual marriage, yet there is no compunction to suffer, "If He desires the soul to suffer, well and good; if not, it doesn't kill itself as it used to." (St. Teresa, p. 439, VII:3:4) Imagine having the capacity to suffer any hardship with repose. Without question our capacity to suffer is directly linked to the degree we are in communion with the divine. Amid difficult circumstances, whenever we are unconscious of the root of our being, we can easily be overwhelmed by discomfort and anxiety. To the extent that we are awake, aware and feeling union with the intimate, infinite presence all around and through us, we are not likely to be disturbed by any set of circumstances.

Hostility towards others is usually a projection of some loss or hurt within ourselves. As a conscious connection to the divine widens and becomes more consistent, hurts and losses naturally dissolve or are for a time dwarfed by the magnitude of the spiritual marriage. Teresa tells us that another effect of spiritual marriage is that the soul can maintain a deep interior joy when persecuted, "without any hostile feelings toward those who do, or desire to do, them evil." (St. Teresa, p. 439, VII:3:5)

Moreover, we learn that another effect of spiritual marriage is that the soul is no longer so eager to die for the Lord but to serve the Lord in a long life. We become detached from everything. One is no longer affected by scorn or praise, desire for achievement or apathy, fear of death or suffering. The soul wants either to be alone (to live a simple life) or be doing something which benefits others. The last effect that Teresa sees for those who realize spiritual marriage is that "There are almost never any experiences of dryness or interior disturbance of the kind that were present at times in all the other dwelling places, but the soul is almost always in quiet." She continues, "There is no reason for the intellect to stir or seek anything, for the Lord who created it wishes to give it repose... I am amazed as well to see that when the soul arrives here all raptures are taken away. Only once in a while are they experienced and then without those transports and that flight of the spirit. They happen very rarely and almost never in public as they very often did before." (St. Teresa, VII:3:2-12) In Zen we say supreme enlightenment is when we no longer depend on or expect enlightenment.

The commentary for the tenth picture begins, "Inside my gate, a thousand sages do not know me. The beauty of my garden is invisible." "Inside my gate" refers to being at home anywhere. The sages do not know me and my garden is invisible because my life has become one of ordinary simplicity. This most natural ordinary state does not stand out, and so is not seen.

"There was a little city, and few men within it; and there came a great king against it, and besieged it, and built great bulwarks against it: Now there was found in it a poor wise man, and he by his wisdom delivered the city; yet no man remembered that same poor man... The words of wise men are heard in quiet more than the cry of him that ruleth among fools." (Ecc. 9:14-17)

"Behold, I send you forth as sheep in the midst of wolves: be ye therefore wise as serpents, and harmless as doves." (Mt. 10:16)

Amma Syncletica said, "Being like serpents means

not ignoring attacks and wiles of the devil [sticky attachments and delusions].... The simplicity of the dove denotes purity of action." (*Desert Fathers*, p. 234)

The second line reads, "Why should one search for the footprints of the ancient masters?" At home with the inner Christ, what more do I need? Anything exterior to this is mere illusion.

"People often say to me: "Pray for me!" Then I think: "Why do you go out of yourselves? Why don't you stay within yourselves and grasp your own blessings? After all, you bear essentially all truth within yourselves." May God help us to be able to remain truly within ourselves in this way, and may he help us to possess all truth immediately and without any distinction! Amen." (Eckhart, p.202)

The last two lines are, "I go to the market place with my gourd and return home with my staff. I visit the wine shop and the market, and everyone I look upon becomes enlightened." With spiritual maturity, one no longer finds living life or preparing for death a hindrance or distraction. Being round instead of square, the mature follower of the Way flows through or around any disturbance. We find natural repose in being useful and of service to others. This would be hard to do if we were to sequester ourselves as hermits permanently. Hence, we return to the marketplace. We bring a caring heart-mind to every action with no effort or cost. The spiritually mature become such natural, clear reflections of the divine that others around them can see their own deep nature.

"In sum, my Sisters, what I conclude with is that we shouldn't build castles in the air. The Lord doesn't look so much at the greatness of our works as at the love with which they are done. And if we do what we can, His Majesty will enable us each day to do more and more, provided that we do not quickly tire. But during the little while this life lasts – and perhaps it will last a shorter time than each one thinks – let us offer the Lord interiorly and exteriorly the sacrifice we can. His Majesty will join it with that which He offered on the cross... Thus even though our works are small they will have the value our love for Him would have merited had they been great." (St. Teresa, p.450, VII:4:15)

All koans, in one way or another, point at this final picture. What follows is the full text of the nineteenth case of the Mumonkan which most directly reflects what this tenth Zen Ox picture and spiritual marriage is all about.

Koan: Ordinary Mind Is Tao [fundamental truth]

Joshu once asked Nansen, "What is Tao?" Nansen answered, "Ordinary mind is Tao." "Then should we direct ourselves toward it or not?" asked Joshu. "If you try to direct yourself toward it, you go away from it," answered Nansen. Joshu continued, "If we don't try, how can we know that it is Tao?" Nansen replied, "Tao does not belong to knowing or to not-knowing. Knowing is illusion; not-knowing is blankness. If you really attain to Tao of no-doubt, it is like the great void, so vast and boundless. How, then, can there be right and wrong in the Tao?" At these words, Joshu was suddenly enlightened.

Mumon's Commentary:

Questioned by Joshu, Nansen immediately shows that the tile is disintegrating, the ice is dissolving, and no communication whatsoever is possible. Even though Joshu may be enlightened, he can truly get it only after studying for thirty more years.

Mumon's Poem:

Hundreds of flowers in spring,
the moon in autumn,
A cool breeze in summer, and snow in winter;
If there is no vain cloud in your mind
For you it is a good season.

How can ordinary mind be Tao? How do we demonstrate this day to day? How do we know when we have realized it? Why will Joshu, even after this breakthrough, truly get it only after studying for thirty more years? In Zen we say enlightenment is as easy as picking up a lump of dirt; on the other hand, spiritual maturity requires decades of work and is always a work in progress. We also say there is nothing to attain and we never arrive.

It is said that before enlightenment, chopping wood and carrying water and after enlightenment, chopping wood and carrying water. Transcending the Trinity, we are free to come down from the mountain of enlightenment and spiritual marriage, back to the bustle and complexities of the market place. With no thought for tomorrow, we are ready to lend a helping hand today. The spiritual journey is not linear, but more like an expanding lumpy spiral going through the interior castle again and again. Remember – enlightenment is easy, spiritual maturity is a never-ending process. Spiritual evolution is not like expanding concentric growth rings, it is more like a growing ameba, alive, in motion, with some aspects more advanced than others and some aspects remaining dark, restricted and perhaps hidden. Only by doing the hard work of using our strengths to see, compost or combust our weaknesses and shortcomings can we foster a wholesome well-rounded development. When we repeatedly walk the labyrinth represented by the Zen Ox pictures, or explore St. Teresa's Interior Castle, we gain a foundation that allows us to lovingly hold and integrate our wounds and primitive instincts for survival. Deeply investigating both our shadow and light, we slowly learn how to empathize with our own and the world's suffering. After many years of meditation practice exploring the inconceivable, we come to accept the inconceivable with equanimity. I think every sage, scientist and philosopher recognizes that any deep question that appears to be answered only leads to ever more profound and unanswerable questions. Regardless, every sage, scientist or philosopher worth their salt, never ceases their perpetual inquiry into the nature of reality.

I don't know why we are here. I don't know why the universe is here. I do recognize that we and the universe itself is miraculous, precious and temporary. Given only this much it becomes imperative to care for our environment and ourselves. As I see it, we are the universe becoming aware of itself! At the very least, it would be foolish to waste this glorious opportunity to explore *who we are and what is This?*

Over the years, as deeper levels are investigated, I've found I can't arrive at any answers. However, I can personally, intimately and genuinely feel the interdependence and the underlying flow of this flowering, unfolding universe. With this feeling, I can't help but make a Great Vow to care for all beings great and small, animate and inanimate.

Perhaps with more practice composting the generational madness handed off to me from my family of origin and my culture, and further digesting the hard knocks that come from living a long life, I will more often rest in the post spiritual marriage represented by the tenth Zen Ox picture. Time will tell. However, I'm not sure any human being can long remain in this state of integration and open heartedness. Our innate complexity is so great that it may be impossible to naturally sustain this seamless openness and selflessness for long. I even question how practical it is to always walk in the world as the holy fool completely free from attachment to rank, position, function, territory, opinions and preferences. And so, until I don't have the mental acuity for more learning, there will always be room for another traverse of the Interior Castle and cycle of the Zen Ox pictures.

GRADUATE SCHOOL IN PSYCHOLOGY (1989 -1991):

My spiritual direction work started in 1988 with informal consultations with three individuals from my two faith communities (Quakers and Zen). Slowly I started seeing more people in one-hour weekly appointments, asking for a small donation. After a year, a dozen people were coming to see me for a modest suggested fee. I realized early in my one-on-one encounters that I did not feel sufficiently capable to assist with some of the more obvious psychological knots that were hindering deeper spiritual exploration. In addition, I felt that I didn't know enough about my own problems, conundrums and complications.

I cannot remember a time when I was not interested in the big questions about life. Why are we here? Where did the universe come from? Does it have a purpose? Do we have a purpose? Why is there suffering? Are there means to mitigate suffering? How much do we universally share? What makes each of us unique? How does the mind work? What ingredients are needed for a functional and creative life? Love is amazing; what is it really? Does love have a common source? What can be done to foster it? Why do all these questions seem important? And, just who is doing the asking? To help myself and others explore these questions more effectively, I started exploring graduate programs in psychology.

I did some volunteer work with the Seattle Mental Health Institute (SMHI) before graduate school. I spent just over a year working with staff and dozens of dual diagnoses (substance abuse and personality disorder) clients, and remain indebted to all of them. It became ever clearer to me that we are all too complicated to grow much on our own without healthy mirroring and mentoring. No one can learn or grow for us; on the other hand, we cannot grow without the support of others.

We do not grow without adversity, loss, disappointment, failures and suffering. My first application was to Seattle University's existential psychology program, but I was not accepted. I remember being bruised not only by the unexpected rejection, but also because it brought up old monsters of self-doubt about my academic ability and worth. Nevertheless, during a quarterly sesshin that immediately followed the rejection notice, I found, despite my swirling emotions, that I was able to enter *samadhi* (harmonious state of awareness) with some consistency. In samadhi all problems of any kind dissolve and a deep equanimity pervades. Without hardship it is hard to grow, with hardship we have the chance to become strong. Moreover, I realized that we can be strong and weak, confused and clear, separate and one, fearful and courageous, right and wrong at the same time.

Shortly afterwards, I was accepted into the graduate psychology program at Antioch University Seattle and began their M.A. program in the fall of 1989. I felt welcomed with open arms. The Antioch program was a good fit for me overall and I graduated in 1991. Could it be that the karmic web (or hands of God) played a part in determining the outcome, or is this just a projection of my mind to protect myself from the random existential realities of the universe? Perhaps the universe is both deterministic and random?! In physics we learn that light is made of indivisible quantum units of energy named photons. Photons behave as particles or waves depending on how they are observed and manipulated. On some fundamental level of reality light is light, yet our best description of light bestows on it two seemingly mutually exclusive properties. Light can be both a particle and a wave because its reality transcends our descriptions. It seems likely that the universe holds many simultaneous contradictory properties. On one level everything in the universe may be predetermined, and yet on another level random and uncertain. When our awareness begins to transcend these descriptions, we begin to learn or relearn how to live in harmony with the universe, with reality, with God and with each other.

The subjects in graduate school that most influenced my training and perspective and opened my eyes to my own early abuse history were the classes on Abuse, Family of Origin, Grief, Developmental Psychology, Object Relations and most importantly a course on Jungian Psychology. In my Jungian Psychology class, I deepened my understanding of how dreams are a gateway to the depths of our unconscious. I've come to see dreams that we remember as post cards from our unconscious. Dreams have compressed multidimensional layers of information that broadcast to our consciousness via the story line, characters and symbols found in them. It is as though there is a universe going on at night that parallels our daytime life. Nightmares and repeating dreams reveal where our own development has hit a snag, and a snag when wound tightly becomes what Jung calls a "complex." In this class, I also began to form in my mind a model of "self" that blends Jung's theory of "the collective unconscious" and the Buddhist concept of *Alaya-vijnana* (seed repository of consciousness). In this model there is no separate discrete self; what we call self is only a self-conscious wave on the surface of a boundless ocean of Mind. In this class I was introduced to the writings of Arnold Mindell, and I was especially moved by one of his books that greatly helped me explore my wounded psyche, *The Shaman's Body*.

During my class on the psychology of grief, a close Quaker friend died of AIDS. Walking the journey with him to the brink of life and death was a very moving experience for both of us. Together, my friend and I came up with some metaphors that helped us get our heads around the transition that was happening. In the first, we are standing with other members of his support committee on the top of a high cliff. Together we all approach the edge of the cliff. It is a sheer drop of more than a hundred feet. Some of the care committee will not get too close to the precipice. Full of trepidation, a few of us stand looking over the edge. We stand there with the "chosen" diver for today, my friend, knowing that only he will have to make the jump, but that sooner or later, with grace or panic, each of us will have our turn. As we look over the cliff, we both note that the water looks warm, clear and even inviting. It is not the water that is the problem; it is the jump that is scary. My friend worries about making a big splash, rather than a smooth entry. He says a big splash might hurt like a belly flop and get the spectators drenched. He says he wants to be the least nuisance to others. I assure him that a little water will not hurt us, and, as for the belly flop, if it happens that way, it can only be the briefest transitory slap, like clapping my hands together. Any way you jump, the water is entered, it is never missed, and this fact is fundamental.

The second metaphor was that of a star descending into a black hole in space. As a collapsing star, my friend begins to recede from this realm of the universe. Space and time are bent like a funnel, warping the area around the collapsing star in such a way that neighboring stars can see the abyss into which one of their own is entering. All of us (neighboring stars) realize that the blackness or void into which one of us falls is the same fate that will one day devour each of us in turn. Moreover, we all are intuitively aware that the void is none other than the dark womb from which we are born. Briefly, while the hole is "open" and our friend still with us, we all become intimately aware of our frailty, our transitory nature, and the foundation or source from which we are born, stand on, and return to. In a few moments, our friend will pass the "event horizon" beyond which no direct communication is possible and the fundamental nature of form metamorphoses into a its essence. Pure union is achieved, the warp snaps back, and space and time are "normal" again, less the light and physical presence of one member, but the gravity of the life lost is still present. Soon all the neighboring stars continue their journey, drift away and begin to forget what they saw, where they came from, where they are going, or what invisibly sustains them. Yet, somewhere, the memory of this encounter adds to the collective unconscious, and hopefully broadens, if only subtly, the "life" of the remaining cluster of friends and family.

About a year after my friend's death, I began volunteering at the newly opened Bailey-Boushay House. This is a hospice house started during the AIDS crisis, that opened its doors in 1992. I was in one of the earliest groups of volunteers to serve there and for a time I led group meditation and sat with patients.

After graduation, I did my required supervision hours under the auspices of one of my advisors, Jeff Skolnick, MD, PhD who is a psychiatrist, mentor and now longtime friend. Jeff is a diplomate of the American Board of Psychiatry and Neurology and a Clinical Assistant Professor of Psychiatry at the University of Washington. He has doctoral training in Neuro-psychology and is author of *Awaken your Brain: Coming Alive to Vibrant Wellness and New Reality.* After my supervision hours were completed, I studied for the national licensing exam and now I am a Licensed Mental Health Counselor (LMHC) in Washington State. I've been working in private practice as a psychotherapist since 1993. My spiritual direction certificate program and two years of graduate school represent only the beginning of my training. Learning from seeing clients and spiritual directees, as well as from peers, peer groups and mentoring was where the real schooling began.

Eventually, between my psychotherapy practice as a licensed mental health counselor and my spiritual direction practice, I was seeing thirty to forty people a week. This continued for two decades. Beginning in 2015 I started seeing at most twenty clients a week. Witnessing the trials and tribulations of so many people has helped me face my own. I'm no use to anyone if I'm not honestly working diligently on my own knots of karmic history. Watching people earnestly soak up their own Inner

Light has encouraged me to keep vigilant in my spiritual disciplines, principally two hours of meditation a day and four or five weeklong silent *sesshins* (meditation intensives) a year. I've been very fortunate, grateful and honored to be included in the spiritual journeys of so many.

Imbued in my work as a spiritual director is the desire to encourage those who come to see me to develop or deepen their relationship to their own spiritual practice. This might be as simple as regularly taking walks in a park, writing poetry, playing a musical instrument, or mindfully and creatively preparing meals. It might mean going to yoga, Tai Chi, doing contemplative prayer, or doing more formal zazen. I invite everyone to name their own path and to deepen it. Some of the questions I always ask on intake are: What was your religious upbringing? What, if anything, do you define as your current spiritual practice? In what kinds of activities do you feel most creative? Please tell me the time or two when you have felt most connected to the divine as you understand it. Or I might ask: Tell me the place, time and activity that was your highest peak experience when you felt in connection with something beyond your ego identity. At successive sessions with me I will ask: How is your practice going? If it is not going so well, I'll ask: What do you think is standing in your way? We all need structure to help us connect to something beyond ourselves. In my view this is the core point of spiritual direction or mentoring –

constantly inviting investigation into beyond the beyond. This is only possible if we ourselves regularly practice swimming in these deep waters.

While exploring spiritual practice with spiritual companions, at some point I will usually share some of what I have learned from the Zen Buddhist perspective about how to deepen one's practice by considering the following three key ingredients: Great Doubt, Great Faith and Great Determination. Great Doubt implies continuous investigation into the two core questions of life: What is *this*? (What is real?) And, who is asking? Great Faith implies basing our practice on our direct experience and experimentation of what works to awaken us to something beyond our personal agenda and sense of self. Great Determination implies developing simple habits to care for our spiritual health, in much the same way as we develop and maintain our personal hygiene. It is also likely that in the course of our work together, I share how the Three Buddhist Treasures (Buddha, Dharma and Sangha) can be used to foster our practice. The Buddha treasure can be used to remember to regularly study the lives of historical sages from any tradition we trust, to commune with spiritual mentors, and regularly consult our own inner sage. The Dharma treasure can be used to remember to study the scriptures, precepts, parables, and queries of the spiritual traditions we trust. The Sangha treasure can be used to remember to associate with a practice community of like-minded seekers. When considered in this way, taking refuge in these three treasures works for any spiritual tradition. On this note, I nearly always encourage those who come to see me to find or deepen an association with a community of practitioners of their choosing.

As a psychotherapist, I work to create sufficient spaciousness and trust to expose sticky wickets, places where people are entangled. Usually there is some arrested development, trauma or abandonment in the past, or some complication of today or even tomorrow, that is getting in one's way. There are many psychological tools that come in handy in exploring and untangling the knots we get ourselves into.

Now that I am a Zen abbot, sometimes people ask, "why don't you cut back further on your spiritual direction and psychotherapy practices?" My answerer is that this work as a counselor keeps me honest, and more importantly it keeps me sane. Constantly helping people work through the places where they get hindered or encumbered, helps me work through my own stuck places. As I listen to things that come out of my mouth, I work to walk my own talk. That keeps me inquiring and exploring.

PSYCHOANALYSIS: WORKING THROUGH EARLY TRAUMA

Beginning when my daughter Adrienne was born in 1983, much of my deep meditation time, especially during sesshins, was plagued by visions of being tortured. For over eight years I had little idea where all these visions and fantasies were coming from. Then with the assistance of MDMA (3,4-Methylenedioxymethamphetamine, commonly known as ecstasy) journeys, I came to the realization that my visions, dreams and fantasies of being tortured were emerging from my early abuse history. While MDMA helped me to regress into my pre-verbal years and appreciate what good and awful experiences were down there, in truth I became psychologically addicted to the "journey," and for a time my MDMA use was excessive. In hindsight my MDMA use saved my life but nearly killed me.

With the encouragement and support of Carolyn and my two psychiatrist friends, I began psychoanalysis with a talented analyst, Dr. Richard Carter, and lay down on my analyst's couch twice a week for three years, from

1993 to 1996. I found Dr. Carter to be a kind soul who looked to me a bit like a big teddy bear. I did not have much negative transference with him; instead, I transferred to him the qualities of my loving maternal step-grandfather who had also been a psychiatrist. Transference occurs when a person redirects some of their feelings or desires for one person to an entirely different person; in therapy, transference happens when a client attaches anger, hostility, love, adoration, or a host of other possible feelings onto their therapist.

At forty years old, through meditation, drugs, acting out, dreams and analysis, I had plumbed the depths of my early history, and the depths were not pretty. I had hoped that by plumbing these depths, miraculously my inner tortured child would go away and leave the adult "me" alone. No such luck. At this point in my life, I was psychologically addicted to MDMA, very depressed and having suicidal thoughts. I realized that the weak adult me was left with the task of reparenting this very damaged kid. Therefore, at forty I slowly started the process of becoming the "foster care father" to this severely abused one-and-a-half-year-old toddler. It has taken most of the last twenty-five years to slowly and lovingly care for this toddler in such a way that "he" trusts "me" to always love and protect him. I have learned that we never lose or outgrow our inner child (there may be more than one). Moreover, each time we take on more responsibilities in life, the cracks and fault lines in our early history again become apparent and must be addressed. As I see it, each successive year adds another story to the building of our life journey. When I was forty, I could see how my early foundational years would require a major earthquake retrofit.

I've already introduced Fred, Jeff and Joseph. I really can't say enough about how all three of them have helped contain my crazy core. Joseph, besides being a spiritual director peer, also comes from an Italian - Irish background with an abusive father. Moreover, he is a Vietnam veteran. Besides his vet buddies, he says I am the only one that he can share his war horror stories with. I'm honored to be included. He too has heard of all my escapades exploring my early trauma. Without his support and love, which helped me to remain safe enough to survive, I might not be here.

Now I will introduce Michele Clarkson, Kate Jacks and Leonard Shaw. Michele is a nationally known sex therapist who shares wisdom and guidance through workshops, public appearances and private practice. She now lives on the Oregon coast and is mostly retired. In 2014 I officiated at her marriage to Charlie Watkins. She has become like a sister to me. We met in a psychotherapy consult group facilitated by Fred Davis, MD that we attended for several years. She too has an early traumatic history which is part of our bond and we hold no secrets from each other.

Kate Jacks, beyond being a social worker, was

trained in massage and movement therapy, and has led workshops on sacred intimacy. We met when she came to me for supervision because I had a reputation for being a therapist with a sex positive attitude. I thought of us as consulting peers, but we did keep regular appointments and there was an exchange of funds, which made it a professional relationship. After a time, I could not hold the strong transference nor the countertransference generated in our meetings; therefore, I initiated the termination of the professional association. Kate and I remain deep friends and our friendship was acutely restorative around my early trauma history.

I met Leonard in a men's psychotherapist consult group about a year after graduate school. After a couple of years in this group, we lost contact. I met him again at a few years ago when he was giving a presentation on his methods at a small gathering of the Puget Sound Adlerian Society. We have since become close buddies, and he has offered, at Chobo-Ji, an annual two-day Spiritually Based Gestalt Workshop where participants experience the blending of Eastern and Western psychology to empower and educate themselves and others. I have also attended intense five-day workshops led by Leonard, and I consider him one of my most loved and trusted spiritual companions. We hold no secrets from each other. I feel so fortunate that I have these seven people in my life with whom I hold no secrets and anything can be examined. With the help of my analyst, partner, and my closest mentors (Fred and Jeff), and my closest peer companions (Joseph, Michele, Kate, and Leonard) the work began and continues. After 1996 I only occasionally went to see Dr. Carter. My last few visits with him were in the summer of 2016. I am grateful that through these key associations that I was able to move far enough along in my exploration and healing of my early trauma to end my addiction to MDMA.

I realize that my work to extricate myself from my corrupted patterns is far from over. Nevertheless, at this point, now 65, I'm cautiously optimistic that I am awake and mature enough to keep my still tangled core wounds from taking over my life or imposing my needs narcissistically on others. The origins of my corrupted patterns undoubtedly are found in my early abuse history and may go back as far as my conception. I will probably never truly be free of them in this lifetime, but I will continue to chip away at my own complexes, hopefully maturing more fully as I go. I'm so grateful for my meditation practice and my closest companions without whom I surely would have been dead long ago. Spiritual practice and spiritual companions point directly to the vastness of our potential to heal, grow, love and transcend our instincts for survival by learning to cultivate true insight, which can only lead to healthy compassionate relations. Wherever we are in our journey of growth and discovery, we are just beginning.

A JOURNEY WITH EIDO TAI SHIMANO
1996 - 2011

In January of 1996 I wrote to Eido Shimano, abbot of Dai Bosatsu Zendo (DBZ) in the Catskill Mountains, about Genki's desire that the Dharma relations between our two temples deepen further with my participation in Holy Days Sesshin at DBZ in April of that year. This was the first of 68 letters that I wrote him in the course of our association, and much of this section is based on a review of these letters which helps me recall significant turns in our relationship.

I attended two sesshins a year at DBZ from this time until the end of my association with Eido. When I began my training with Eido Shimano I had heard stories of his improprieties with multiple women Sangha members, but I foolishly thought he had reformed his ways. I continued to believe that until new revelations came to light in 2010. Shortly after this, I stopped training with him.

During that first sesshin at DBZ I had three breakthroughs that helped loosen some knots from my early history. Being in Eido's presence at this remote, traditional Zen monastery re-stimulated some very old fears and shames around my relationship to my father. Eido was both kind and stern. He always had a *keisaku* (waking stick) in front of him during dokusan, which he used regularly to strike his students to encourage them. I told him at our first dokusan meeting that he was never to strike me because it would be confused with the cruelty that my father inflicted on me. Because he kindly honored this request and never beat me or ridiculed me as I had seen him do to others, I developed a huge positive transference towards him. In my psyche he became a good father figure. However, even with this positive transference, in the early years of our association I felt more frightened around him than I could recall ever feeling around anyone. I recognized that I had a deep need for approval from father figures in my life, and that this need turned into fear that I wouldn't be accepted or approved, but I never felt this intensity of fear with any of my other Zen teachers. I believe this was because, of all my Zen teachers, he was the most like my father.

My training with Eido helped me to appreciate the strengths and limitations of my training with Genki. From Genki I could learn the quintessential teaching of Zen practice: Daily life is the enlightened life. Zazen (seated meditation) is the seed that gives rise to the plant of *samu* (work meditation), mindfully folding the laundry, making a bed, sweeping a floor, preparing a meal, washing the dishes, working in the garden, arranging flowers, whisking a bowl of tea.... The fruit of zazen is an open heart, caring for all beings, great and small, animate and inanimate. For all Genki's faults, in his daily life (except for rare and sometimes glaring exceptions) he demonstrated these truths throughout the day, and I'm ever so grateful for his teaching. Genki also demonstrated how daily life is meant to be a creative life. He was an amazing cook, dedicated potter, gardener, writer, and calligrapher. Because of the language barrier, his English was never very good, so he could not teach me the subtle nuances of koans. However, he was able to invite me to respond non-verbally to koans, which is the foundation of koan training. Students are taught to approach koans by identifying with a key element of the parable or story and then communing with that element until an insight bubbles up for testing before the Zen master. It is nearly always best that one's first presentation be non-verbal. For example, if the key element in a koan is the sound of rain, how would one present the essence of rain without words? As a hint, we are asked to first consult our inner seven-year-old for a nonverbal response, then temper this response with the wisdom of our inner sage and combine the two to make a demonstration without words. Working with Genki in this arena, because of his poor English language skills, forced me to learn how to respond like a good mime.

After this initial response a Zen master will ask, "What does that mean?" Here Genki and I could only go so far. Under the guidance and care of Glenn Webb and Hirano Osho-san I opened my Zen eye, with Genki's guidance I learned how to see and be in the world around me, but because Genki's English was limited it was like seeing the world without my glasses on. Under the tutelage of Eido Shimano, who had mastered the English language, I was able to work into the depth of koans, which was like learning how to see the world with my glasses on.

After my second sesshin with Eido, I wrote him a letter about waiting in the DBZ dokusan line and while there seeing a picture of him, as a younger man, sitting alone in the zendo. I remember that at every dokusan encounter I was nervous to meet with him; at the time, I so wanted his approval. Seeing him in this painting, sitting utterly alone from others, but not separate from the wider world and the flow of Dharma, gave me peace of mind. I imagined that I too could sit this way and not be disturbed. Often in a zendo, sitting with many others, each practitioner has the feeling of being entirely alone but not at all lonely. Deep sitting eventually brings us into harmony with beyond the beyond, which feels like a formless but ubiquitous, all embracing loving presence. When doing contemplative prayer or seated meditation, especially at a silent retreat or weeklong sesshin, our awareness expands and deepens. Through this practice the artificial walls that normally separate our sense of self from our sense of other slowly become transparent or may temporarily dissolve completely. Buddhism describes a spectrum of consciousness that begins with awareness of our five senses, then deepens into a persistent sense of self-awareness (ego consciousness), which may deepen with practice to awareness of the *Alaya-vijnana* ("seed" repository – corresponding to Carl Jung's idea of the collective unconscious). If we go deeper still, we may experience pure consciousness, an awareness unrelated to self-identity, an awareness that embraces the universe.

I first came upon the Buddhist concept that distinguishes classes of consciousness in *The Three Pillars of Zen*, by Philip Kapleau. The following description of ten levels is based on my own interior experience of consciousness that moves from what may be called relative awareness to absolute awareness, or from personal mind to universal Mind. During extended periods of contemplation, from time to time our concrete personal awareness will fade and a more subtle and universal awareness will blossom. No matter how many years we have practiced, I suspect that most of the time we never get beyond the first three levels. This is certainly true for me.

Ten Levels of Consciousness

1) Bodily Awareness: often we are subtly or actively aware of reports from our circulatory, nervous, respiratory, digestive, sensory, and ambulatory systems. Moreover, unless we are sleeping, we are nearly always aware of what is being reported by our five senses.

2) Self Awareness: It is hard not to be aware of our core ego identity, and mostly aware of our sub-personas related to our roles, positions, history, education, gender identity, sexual orientation and everything else in our awake psychological wardrobe.

3) Superego Awareness: we recognize the inner voices of our internalized good mother, bad mother, good father, bad father, and all the voices of our known significant others, teachers, mentors and tormentors.

4) Shadow Awareness: we start to become aware of our far less known ancestors, and of closeted or denied aspects of our selves, such as opposite gender, or different sexual attractions and orientations. If we view ourselves as good, we may be denying our beastly aspects. We deny these aspects out of fear that if expressed, they might take over and appear as a molester, rapist, abuser, even a mass murderer. If we view ourselves as a bad beast, we may well be missing that we are also

loving bodhisattvas (sages that care for all beings).
5) Awareness of Archetypes: Sage, Innocent, Explorer,
Ruler, Creator, Caregiver, Magician, Hero, Outlaw, Lover,
Jester, Victim, Perpetrator, Child, Adolescent, Parent,
Priest, Priestess, Witch, Wizard... The names are not
important. If we listen and observe carefully enough, we
can all feel various kinds of decidedly human archetypal
currents pulling and pushing us.

6) Totem Awareness: Owl, Bear, Deer, Raven, Orca,
Snake, Eagle, Lion, Lamb, Wolf... Again, the names are
not important. If we listen and observe carefully enough,
we can all feel various kinds of animal archetypal currents
guiding or influencing us.

7) Awareness of Fundamental Nature: Ice, Sun, Star,
Moon, Fog, Rain, Ocean, Tree, Grass, Rock... Going
ever deeper into our own true nature we become aware
and in awe of every leaf, blade of grass and grain of sand.

8) Awareness of Fundamental Polarities: 4-elements
(earth/wind – fire/water), 4-directions (North/South –
East/West), Yin/Yang, Male/Female, Hot/Cold, Alive/
Dead... Moving way down into our collective unconscious
we can feel the fundamental polarities of this alive multi-
dimensional universe.

9) Awareness of the Tao of No Name: This is where we

dissolve into the intimate, infinite, flow of the Dharma, the flowering, fundamental essence of the universe, prior to heaven and earth, prior to the Big Bang, incomparably profound and minutely subtle, and vocalized as *Mu* in Rinzai Zen.

10) Tathagata's Awareness: Tathagata is a name Gautama Buddha used in referring to himself that means, "the one who has thus gone." When and if we can let go of any awareness of ego-identity by falling or dissolving into the intimate, infinite, vast, bottomless void of our deep nature, then awareness of the embracing presence of the universe becomes apparent. This loving presence is always everywhere and is everything. It has no form, no birth, no death, let alone a name.

Please remember that with all the awareness or enlightenment possible, one may still act badly if there is little maturity. Furthermore, there are many mature individuals who unknowingly live lives as bodhisattvas, who have little explored the reality of their deep nature. Awakening is much easier to come by than maturity. Awakening may give us the depth and breadth of consciousness to grow and mature; on the other hand, it can also give us the ability to use our awareness to spiritually bypass the need for maturity, which of course ends up being very problematic.

In July of 1997, Genki Takabayashi moved from Seattle to Montana. This move also meant that for all intents and purposes, I was the *de facto* abbot of the Seattle Zen temple. In the fall of 1997, during my attendance at Harvest Sesshin at DBZ, I had a deep encounter with the wind. The wind was very blustery and howling during the last night. At the time I was working the koan "Partakers of Brewer's Grain." In this koan Zen Master Obaku states, "I didn't say there was no Zen, just no one who teaches Zen." I sat that night fully absorbed by Obaku's statement. Sitting in the zendo an insight suddenly penetrated every cell of my being. I realized that no one teaches the wind how to blow or howl! And thought, "I did not say there was no wind, just that there is no one who teaches the wind." Rarely do insights dawn on me suddenly, usually they bubble to the surface of my consciousness slowly passing through many filters. Each aspect of the universe is completely unique and always seamless with all things seen and unseen. There is no one who can teach the Tao anything. There is no one who has ever directed the wind. There is no mind running the universe. There is just No-Mind which is marvelously alive and growing spontaneously as this universe. As Eido often said, "When you give yourself wholeheartedly to the Dharma, the Dharma gives itself to you."

I led my first Seattle sesshin in March of 1998. Genki was in attendance briefly, but deferred all leadership to me. I had the strong feeling that all my teachers and mentors were standing with me and informing me about how to lead throughout the week. Moreover, I could feel the Zen lineage come up deep within and push me forward in the direction I needed to go. This is a wonderful feeling, but often I felt that I was being pushed too far ahead of the wave; in other words, I felt as though I was just going along for the ride and that my insight was far ahead of my maturity, which was true. Fortunately, over time there seems to be less discrepancy between what is said and who is saying or doing it. My closing incense poem for this first sesshin was as follows:

> Over vast Plum Mountain,
> a fresh spring rain falls.
> A new beginning together,
> with old Dharma friends.
> Opening the gateless gate,
> who enjoys the view?
> The crows dance and squawk,
> building their new nest.

Contemplative prayer or zazen in our daily life is like water given to the desert, but if our practice isn't guided by values and principles associated with respect and care of all beings, we are sure to go astray. By the fall of 1998 plans were being made by Eido and Genki to install me officially as Chobo-Ji's second abbot.

In the autumn of 1998, I returned from my eighth

sesshin at DBZ. I wrote Eido, "For some reason, digesting and combusting my under-processed personal history waited for a meeting with you at DBZ." My journals for most of my fourteen years of training at DBZ are full of revelations about how my early traumatic history and intense fears had and were continuing to influence my life. Nevertheless, there was a shift after I gave a Dharma talk during DBZ's 1998 Harvest Sesshin. Something cathartic happened for me. It was as if a veil of confusion temporarily lifted and I felt freer than I had ever felt before. For a time, everything in my life felt stronger, clearer, and happier than I could ever remember. For a while, I felt I was never far from deep-seated equanimity.

I was installed as Chobo-Ji's second abbot and named as a Zen Dharma Teacher (*Zenji*) on January 10, 1999 in Seattle. At the ceremony, I spoke of my great gratitude to Genki and Eido for their care and patience with me as their student and vowed to endlessly continue my training in Zen. I said to those gathered at the ceremony, "Together we have become a kind of transition group from the East to the West. Right here and now we have made this remarkable commitment to continue a tradition that comes to us from across the Pacific, and to make it work here in the United States as our own." I concluded with, "When in 1955 Eido Roshi and Genki Roshi met at their first sesshin together, and, for some reason, sat next to each other, neither having the faintest idea if they were both end up in America, I was one year old. They were sitting zazen next to each other, while I was a toddler in Los Angeles. Genki Roshi has often made it known that just now, he is beginning to understand; just now he is beginning to do deep Zen practice. I am also very fond of this sentiment, for I too just now have the feeling that I am beginning to practice deeply. And, I hope that in each successive year I feel the same way."

In June of 2000, I attended a remarkable meeting of international Buddhist teachers at Spirit Rock, an Insight Meditation Center in Woodacre, California. There I met for the second time the Dalai Lama, and for the first time Jack Kornfield, Ram Dass and Bodhin Kjolhede. Jack Kornfield is widely known in American Buddhist circles and I have long been a fan of his writing. He was the host of this gathering, so I got to know him a bit. I was amazed that he knew of Genki Takabayashi and his story in Seattle. It seemed to me that Jack knows everybody. One of Jack's books that I greatly admire, read in 1993 and wish I had written is *A Path with Heart: A Guide Through the Perils and Promises of Spiritual Life*. Ram Dass arrived in a wheel chair as it was not that long after his major stroke in 1997. I was moved by his courageous efforts at recovery, and his ability to embrace change, aging and dying. The book of his that most influenced me is *How Can I Help? Stories and Reflections on Service*. Bodhin sought me out at this conference because we were both deep students of Zen koans. Bodhin is the Dharma successor of Roshi Philip Kapleau and is the Abbot and Director of the Rochester Zen Center. He was ordained a Buddhist priest in 1976, four years before I was. He and I have maintained friendship and mutual admiration since then. We have been at many meetings together and will spontaneously call one another for consultation and encouragement.

My time at DBZ with Eido was very often a wild and crazy ride from terror to "enlightenment" and back again. Often getting on a plane to go to DBZ I felt like I was being transported to a maximum-security prison to be put to death. Once the sesshin started I usually could find a groove of deep samadhi. One bright night sitting in the middle of Harvest (Autumn) Sesshin in 2000 I wrote in my journal, "Tonight, I had the odd feeling that I was a Zen forest monk long ago, feeling the same cold, seeing the same moon, in complete repose with forest, mountains and waters. No need to teach anything, but a desire to share with others the peace of having nowhere to go and nothing to do. Somehow it really seems like we are all meant to live this way. Perhaps Zen is just way ahead of its time, or perhaps Zen practice represents the early stages of a new dawn. It matters not whether I was the forest monk at one time or another; however, it feels so good to know the timeless nature of equanimity."

At one of the early Rohatsu sesshins (longest and most intense Zen retreat of the year) I led there were more than thirty participants with me at Camp Indianola on the Kitsap Peninsula, on the shores of Puget Sound. Three people in attendance that year became deep Dharma friends who have seen me through thick and thin: Rodger Tozan Park, Steve Shinkai Garber and Ken Eklund. I haven't spoken to Tozan in a few years, but I used to make an annual trip to his Dojo in Ann Arbor, Michigan to lead a three-day sesshin for his Aikido students. Rodger was one of many senior students of Chief Birankai Instructor, Chiba Sensei, who was a close friend of Genki's. Steve, also a long-time student of T. K. Chiba Sensei, fairly regularly attends a sesshin in Seattle and is nearly always at my annual three-day sesshin in San Diego. Sadly, Ken succumbed to ALS on August 6, 2018. He and I had been friends for more than 30 years. We once lived in the Seattle PRAG collective house together. Ken was an environmental attorney and voraciously lived life to the fullest right to the end.

I sometimes refer to Zen as an extreme sport religion. In my view, all spiritual companions, spiritual mentors and spiritual directors should attend at least one silent week-long contemplative retreat a year; moreover, it is my opinion they should be encouraging anyone who consults with them to do the same. A contemplative silent retreat need not be as arduous as a Zen sesshin, but without at least a week each year to untangle ourselves, I don't see how spiritual growth is possible.

Bob Heiwa Burns Sensei was another close spiritual companion, picked me up in Newark, New Jersey for my DBZ Sesshins. Bob was another senior student of Aikido T. K. Chiba Sensei. He had already attended many Rohatsu Sesshins with me in Seattle and continued to train with me until his untimely death in July of 2017. Before going on to DBZ I would often stop at his Aiki Farms Dojo and stay two nights and lead a one-day *zazenkai* (short silent zazen retreat). He grew up on a farm in Ledyard, CT and lived across the street from his childhood home. Bob had joined the U.S. Marine Corps after high school. After leaving the Marines, he taught martial arts at a Marine

Corps recruit depot, trained wild horses, acted in the New York theater scene, lived on a boat in the Virgin Islands, and ended up running the small Aikido Dojo and organic farm in Ledyard. When he took the Buddhist Precepts with me in October of 2011, I gave him the Dharma name Heiwa, which means Soldier of Peace. Some would say he was very temperamental and cantankerous. He was someone with whom I could confide my early trauma history and know he would not judge me for my acting out, yet he was never afraid to point out my weaknesses and offer concrete suggestions. Most of all he trusted me to find my way, and I trusted that he would find his own way too. He always recognized my warrior spirit, as did my two Vietnam veteran friends (Joseph Cospito and Claude Anshin Thomas). Bob was one of my dozen deep spiritual companions and he is sorely missed.

One DBZ Memorial Day Sesshin, in May of 2002, ended in a spectacular blaze of thunder and shame. I think Eido thought I needed to be taken down a few notches; perhaps he thought that I was being a bit arrogant, which is hard not to do whenever one moves up in a hierarchy. Anyway, during the last daily Sangha officer meeting of this retreat, I spoke up and made a comment about how impressed I was by the post holders (temple officers) running the sesshin so smoothly. I said something like what an honor it was to witness the quality of their efforts to support all participants. I then further related how I would honor Eido's Dharma Grandfather, Yamamoto

Gempo Roshi's upcoming annual memorial in Seattle with specific chants. Neither of these statements sat well with Eido. First, Eido was angry that I saw myself as only a witness of his sesshin. Second, in my ignorance, I quoted the wrong memorial chants for a Dharma Ancestor. He said nothing in the officer meeting, but by the time he gave his last Teisho of sesshin, he blew a gasket and ripped me a new one. He told everyone in so many words what a nincompoop I was. This certainly took me down a few pegs and I was literally shaking with both dread and embarrassment from his thunder.

Spiritual leaders of any kind are bound to attract transference of old family of origin dynamics that will be projected as idealizations or negative expectations and intentions. This is unavoidable. The more difficult the student's developmental history, the stronger the transference will be and the harder it will be to resist responding with countertransference (an emotional reaction to the transference that may be as strong as love or hate). I think my transference was contributing to Eido's thunder. I wrote him a letter of apology. Eido wrote back that he read my letter multiple times, accepted my apology, and our training together continued.

In September of 2002, Roko Sherry Chayat (aka Shinge Roko Roshi), a Dharma Heir of Eido Shimano and abbot of the Zen Center of Syracuse (Hoen-Ji), led a half-day retreat at Chobo-Ji in Seattle. Roko and I sat many sesshins together at DBZ and she invited me to join the American Zen Teachers Association (AZTA) where we got to know each other better at the very collegial annual meetings. She started her Zen training with Eido Shimano and his teacher Soen Nakagawa Roshi in 1967; I began my training in 1975. She was born in 1943, eleven years my senior. She was ordained an unsui in 1985, by Maurine Stuart (a student of Soen Roshi from Canada), four years after I was ordained by Genki. She had shifted from Eido to Maurine because of his sexual shenanigans with Sangha members, but returned to him after Maurine died in 1990. In 1996 Roko edited a book of the teachings of Maurine, *Subtle Sound*, which is one of the most down-to-earth books on Zen I have read. Roko was given teaching permission in 1992 and then Dharma Transmission by Eido Shimano in 1998, making her the first American woman to receive transmission in the Rinzai School. I saw her as my elder Dharma sister and had deep respect for her clarity, dignity and maturity as a Zen practitioner. In her Teisho that day in 2002 at Chobo-Ji, she began "It's a great pleasure to be here, to sit with all of you, to join my dear Dharma brother, to be in the lap of Buddha Dharma in Seattle." For a good while we were deep spiritual companions for each other, but later fell out of each other's confidence. In our early years together, I often confided in her with great trust.

In August of 2003, I attended a memorable annual meeting of the AZTA, held in Rochester, New York, with twenty-six second generation Zen teachers (first generation teachers came from Asia) from around the country. One day Roko and I circumambulated the lake on the Chapin Hill Zen property, and took a dip together. During a side trip, I briefly participated in an intimate small meeting with Roshi Philip Kapleau. He was greatly disabled by Parkinson disease, and it was very difficult for him to communicate. Nevertheless, his spirit was shining strongly and I felt honored to have briefly been with him before his death the following year. He wrote many books, none more famous than *The Three Pillars of Zen*, which as a young man in college I had devoured. This book along with *Zen Mind, Beginner's Mind* by Shunryu Suzuki, inspired me to pursue Zen training. This meeting was also a chance to renew and deepen my connection to Bodhin Kjolhede. During this trip to New York, Roko invited me to make a trip to her temple, Hoen-Ji, the Zen Center of Syracuse. There I met and spoke with the gathered Syracuse Sangha and my admiration for Roko and the intensity of her work to foster authentic Zen training deepened.

For a few years around this time, I began to lead annual three-day sesshins in Strasbourg, France and later Birmingham, England. These were organized by senior students of Chief Birankai Aikido instructor Chiba Sensei. In England the retreats were hosted by Chris Gyoshin Mooney Sensei, who is a delightful spiritual companion of mine, and has an amazing wit and joyous presence that I much admire.

In November of 2004, I invited Claude AnShin Thomas, a Vietnam War veteran and Zen unsui ordained in 1995 by Tetsugen Bernard Glassman of the Zen Peacemaker Order, to speak at Chobo-Ji. Claude served as a gunner in an assault helicopter and, like my friend Joseph Cospito, had killed many Vietnamese people. Both Joseph and Claude, along with most other war veterans, suffered from PTSD after the war. In the early 1990s, Claude worked to settle his PTSD by attending a retreat with Thich Nhat Hanh, a Vietnamese Zen Priest. The talk at Chobo-Ji was powerful and helped us all reflect on how we are living our lives. He talked about his newly released book, *At Hell's Gate: A Soldier's Journey from War to Peace.* AnShin and I began a correspondence after this meeting that continues to this day. I consider him one of my deepest Dharma brothers. When I feel confused or conflicted, he is on the short list of people I will call.

In 2006 I attended DBZ's Anniversary Sesshin. This was to join the thirty-year anniversary celebration of the opening of DBZ, which took place on July 4, 1976. At the Anniversary Sesshin, Eido pushed me hard to commit to becoming the next Vice Abbot and heir apparent to the Zen Study Society (ZSS) temples, DBZ and NYZ. To assume this responsibility, I would need to move to New York. This would mean moving my family, leaving my home Sangha in Seattle, closing my private psychotherapy practice, and leaving my support system of close friends. It would make it more difficult to visit and support Genki in his retirement and necessitate becoming a full-time priest and monk. Carolyn had already emphatically told me that she would not come with me! Moreover, I've already alluded how difficult it was to get on a plane to attend DBZ sesshins. Imagine how much harder it would be to board a plane knowing that I would be permanently moving to New York.

As you might imagine, I was struggling mightily with the call to move to New York. The last night of sesshin, I entered a dark night of the soul. During the long sit just before the conclusion of scheduled sitting, there was a shift in my inner landscape. My attachment to everything important to me temporarily fell away. I have had similar experiences before, but not to this depth. What was extraordinarily new about this shift was that I broke through any attachment to Eido's approval, which meant that I had lost any attachment to advancement. Suddenly, I no longer cared about achieving Dharma Transmission or becoming one of Eido's Dharma Heirs. Moreover, I blew through my attachment to ritual, form, and doctrine. I wrote a verse that expressed my opening on a napkin and brought it to Eido's *Inji* (temple attendant) who passed it on to him that evening.

I then returned to the zendo and sat most of the night on my own, processing what this insight might mean going forward. In the midst of great exhaustion and pain there was light, easy, clear openheartedness. I realized that I would go with the wind. If I was really needed in New York, so be it. The next morning, Eido Roshi was very happy. I told him the shift meant that I no longer needed to cling to the "good life" I had in Seattle. In other words, if circumstances necessitated a move to New York, then what would be would be. Eido said, "You have obligations to Genki Roshi and the Seattle Sangha which would have to be worked out," and I agreed.

After my return home to Seattle, I told Carolyn about my breakthrough and after hearing this account, she acquiesced and said that if I was going to move to New York, she too would come. Had I lost my mind? I didn't know, but I was willing to give up everything to further the development of Rinzai Zen in the West. My love for Eido was at its height. I very much wanted to train with him for as long as possible, knowing full well that I no longer needed him or anyone to be my teacher. My own unfolding was now sufficiently rooted that further practice and exploration could continue without dependence on a teacher.

Plans began to be made for my Dharma Transmission Ceremony, which would take place in the spring of 2008. Eido, Genki, Roko and others began arriving in Seattle on May 20, 2008 in preparation for the May 21 *Shiho Shiki* (Dharma Transmission - *Inka*) Ceremony. Shortly after their arrival a traditional Japanese whisked green-tea ceremony was held at Bonnie Mitchell Sensei's home overlooking Lake Union. That night there was a celebratory dinner at the Nishino Japanese Restaurant.

The morning of the 21st the Chobo-Ji Sangha met for meditation and then moved the whole zendo to the University Friends Quaker Meeting (UFM) Worship Room, which could accommodate all those expected for the 11 a.m. ceremony. The Social Hall at UFM was set up for a delicious white tablecloth lunch buffet that followed the ceremony.

At the ceremony I offered the following verse:

The Buddha, Dharma and Sangha are all empty.
What is there to treasure?

There is nothing to attain.
What can be transmitted?

Digesting entanglements,
Body and Mind are set free.

Nothing to do but listen
to the thunder
And follow the wind.

During the ceremony four senior peers acted as gatekeepers: Richard Zenshin Rudin, Genchoku Johnson, Zenmu Brenda Nightingale, and Genko Kathy Blackman. Each poised a spiritual question that had to be answered spontaneously in order to pass to the next gate. Also present and seated in the front row were my mother, daughter, Michele Clarkson, Kate Jacks, Fred Davis, Joseph Cospito, and Ken Eklund. These last five along with Carolyn will always remain in my heart as my closest spiritual companions. The verse was a slightly modified version of the insight poem I had shared with Eido the last night of the 2006 Anniversary Sesshin at DBZ. On that day in 2008 I joined a lineage of 83 Dharma ancestors which began with the historical Buddha. However, one should not take this association too seriously. For one thing, as Eido often pointed out, the 83rd copy of something can only be a rather degraded facsimile of the original. Secondly, the whole idea of the lineage association was concocted by the Chinese because of the necessity to demonstrate Confucian filial piety for one's ancestors. What I do take seriously is my faith that at the ground of our being we all share one Mind that has no dependence on form or time.

That night there was a dinner with sixty people at Ivar's Salmon House. At this dinner John Daijo Lowrance, a Chobo-Ji Sangha member for more than ten years, took me aside and told me that he wanted to support the temple's move and expansion into a residential practice center. After much search and consideration, the Zen House (our meeting place for the previous 13years) was sold and Chobo-Ji's Residential Practice Center had its opening ceremony on Oct. 8, 2011.

Frankly, I wouldn't wish this Dharma Heir – Abbot role on my worst enemy. The higher the position the greater the transference and countertransference. I learned all about transference in graduate school, and then learned much more about it in my consult group with Fred Davis, in my men's psychotherapist group, and most of all from working with psychotherapy clients. As a spiritual director I see directees once a month, and there is very little transference. Seeing clients once and sometimes twice a week as a psychotherapist generates a lot more transference. Being a preceptor, residential guide and abbot who ordains and oversees unsui (novice Zen priest) training, and leads four weeklong marathon meditation retreats a year exponentially generates transference and countertransference.

Chobo-Ji offers meditation services every day of the week, and every day I am expected to show up and help lead the services. This is both a blessing and a curse. It is a blessing because the expectations of my role necessitate a lot of meditation, which generally keeps my personal craziness in check. It is a curse, because seeing people this often and with such intensity sets up projections and idealistic expectations. Moreover, because of countertransference I am tempted to fall into inappropriate parental or significant friend attitudes towards fellow followers of the Way. Another form of countertransference is either to believe the idealization of others, which leads to arrogance and a false sense of self-importance, or to feel crushed by criticism, doubt, projections or disapproval. I must always be aware of these temptations, ward them off the best I can and get consultation with either peers or mentors when having trouble. I have two key Zen Buddhist peers, AnShin and Bodhin, and a few more that I consult with as needed. In addition, I have several local close professional friends to draw from. Most of the time warding off countertransference temptations is a breeze; nevertheless, because transference and countertransference are more pronounced as I progress on the Way, it is the hardest part of my calling. It is this aspect of my role that requires the most skillful means. Therefore, I must continue to cultivate and deepen my skillfulness year after year.

In my view hierarchy in a spiritual formation structure is necessary. We need mentors and guides who have preferably decades of experience to help mirror and gently prod our unfolding. We are after all the most complex creatures not only on this planet, but quite possibly in a whole quadrant of the galaxy. Rocks and trees need no guidance; however, the more sophisticated an animal is, the longer the interval of parenting needs to be. In the case of humans, we outgrow the need for our parent's counsel as young adults, but we still need much more subtle mirroring to fully flower into maturity. Moreover, deep individuation requires that we push through and transcend the artificial barriers that are set up between a teacher and student. In Zen training the teacher is in the role of host and the student in the role of guest. We say there is Dharma Transmission when host recognizes host; in other words, the student has achieved or surpassed the teacher's understanding and maturity.

There is nothing like hierarchy based on religion to stimulate transference. This is because religious hierarchy directly stimulates the conscious and unconscious recollection of the power disparity found in every family between parents and children. If the natural power disparity in one's family of origin is not smoothly resolved during maturation to young adulthood, or worse parents abdicate or abuse their authority, then entanglements are sure to ensue. Family of origin entanglements will manifest as arrested or incomplete development. These issues will then be brought to the next hierarchical relationship, which is often the church, synagogue or temple. This was certainly true in my relationship with Eido Shimano and has been true for some who have come to train with me. This is to be expected, and is not something to reject or judge as bad. Many of my issues with my dead biological father were slowly worked through by seeing and digesting the projections, attachments, and expectations I brought into my relationships with Genki and Eido.

The dokusan (personal interview) room is a place where artificial hierarchy is on steroids. There are two bows entering and two bows exiting. The host is dressed up in fancy robes and has a *keisaku* (waking stick) at the ready. The purpose (and, I'm very clear to everyone about this) is to stimulate any residual fear associated with hierarchy and disappointing authority figures. Courageously facing these fears, the guest learns at a minimum to better manage them and at best completely combusts them. In time the aura of the power differential is transcended, and the guest, through repeated dokusan encounters, gains confidence, spontaneity, flexibility and access to insight. And when the guest sees behind the curtain of artificial hierarchy, two people become both host and guest for each other, and often there is a lot of laughter.

Undoubtedly, every relationship that has soured between a fellow follower of the Way and me after assuming Zen leadership has involved some measure of transference and countertransference. Sometimes the transference is much greater than the countertransference; other times, and I hope more rarely, countertransference has played a more significant role. You can never find one without the other and at every turn I regret not being more skillful.

It is important to realize that each of us already has an inner sage that is always there, but not always seen. Our spiritual practices help us cultivate recognition and confidence in this inner sage. However, gaining recognition and confidence is only half the battle. The most difficult task is to allow this inner sage to consistently direct our actions. Often our egocentric personal agenda and preferences trumps our inner sage, or worse we fool ourselves into believing that our egocentric agenda is the Inner Master that must be followed. This confusion becomes deeper when our personal history has more wounds and entanglements.

DISILLUSION AND DISSOLUTION

Unbeknownst to me when I began to train with Eido in 1996, a letter had been written to the then Board President of the ZSS Richard Zenshin Rudin, dated Aug. 9, 1995 and authored by seven prominent American Zen teachers. It began, "We write to you as colleagues of your teacher, Eido Shimano, Roshi, and as your fellow students in the Maha-Sangha [wide Buddhist community] in North America. Our concern in this letter is the Buddha Dharma and the well-being of the women and men who invest themselves in its practice. Over the past three decades, we have interviewed many former students of Shimano Roshi. Their stories are consistent: trust placed in an apparently wise and compassionate teacher, only to have that trust manipulated in the form of sexual misconduct and abuse. Some of these students elected to continue their practice with us; most of them wanted nothing further to do with Zen Buddhism. With report after report of the same depressing story, it is clear to us that our colleague Shimano Roshi, is not simply one who slips into an occasional love affair. We have no hesitation in judging from first-hand accounts that the quality of these relationships is not loving but exploitative and extremely damaging to his victims." I would like to think that if I had been aware of this letter before I started training with Eido, I would have never started. I first read this letter in 2009, with much additional material, on the shimanoarchive.com. This is a compilation of material published on the internet by a Dharma brother, Kobutsu Malone. Kobutsu drew substantially on the Robert Aitken Archives held at the University of Hawaii. I wouldn't come to know Kobutsu for some years, and regrettably never met him in person before his death in 2019. In June of 2010 a scandal broke about Eido Shimano having yet another sexual liaison with a female student. This was a pattern of inappropriate behavior that I thought had concluded before I began to train with him in 1996. Immediately pressure was put on Eido to resign from the Board of the Zen Studies Society (ZSS), which has the legal and fiduciary responsibility for the two ZSS properties, Dai Bosatsu Zendo (DBZ) in the Catskill Mountains and the New York City center, Shobo-Ji. This was done so that the extent of his ethical breach could be fully investigated before any further remedies were sought. Eido resigned from the ZSS Board July 4th, 2010. I was a board member of ZSS at the time.

To assist with the ethics investigation the ZSS Board enlisted the help of the FaithTrust Institute, a Seattle-based group skilled at such work. What was discovered over the course of months was credible evidence that the most recent incident was not the only breach of ZSS ethical guidelines. We often heard Eido claim that this sort of behavior ended many years ago. In fact, what we learned was that over the course of decades, Eido abused his position of power and authority repeatedly, and was in the habit of aggressively pursuing the most vulnerable, attractive female students under his spiritual care. In addition, it became increasingly clear that his many so-called apologies over the years reflected no serious understanding of the harm he had done. Most disturbing of all was hearing a credible first-person account that not all sexual encounters were started "consensually," and the fact that he transmitted STDs to his own students.

Eido Roshi resigned as Abbot of ZSS on December 8, 2010. Eido designated Shinge Roko Sherry Chayat, my senior Dharma sister, to be installed as the new abbot on January 1, 2011. I thought this was a good move on Eido's part because ZSS could best be served with a woman at the helm. In February 2011, ZSS announced that Eido would no longer teach Zen under their auspices. After the scandal broke in June 2010, five ZSS board members, including myself, had resigned because we became frustrated with the board's inability to more aggressively address the magnitude of Eido's failings. Three different meetings were held to give the ZSS Sangha a chance to voice their concerns; the most recent was a weekend late in August 2011. I wanted to attend this meeting but was turned back by Hurricane Irene. Much was accomplished at this meeting, but in my mind so much more needed to be done to serve those who had been harmed.

Late in 2011, I asked the Chobo-Ji board to consider terminating our affiliation with ZSS. After two months of deliberation, when it became clear that ZSS was ready to move on without taking further steps to address those Sangha members who had been most harmed or alienated by Eido's behavior, the Chobo-Ji Board wrote a letter requesting that Chobo-Ji be removed from their listing of Related Zen Centers.

My mind and heart went through periods of anger, frustration, disappointment and doubt concerning my long association with Eido and ZSS, but I have learned some invaluable lessons. First and foremost among them is that meditation practice can indeed nurture true insight, but true insight alone, especially when bounded by a bubble of arrogance and self-aggrandizement, is insufficient for deep maturity in the Way. Genuine maturity requires that we examine our lives and vow to root out any repeating pattern or program that harms others. We must always be on the lookout for patterns that cause harm. These patterns represent gaps in our development and we must vow to expose, examine and face our shortcomings so thoroughly that they are transformed from liabilities to assets. This effort will likely be the hardest and most important work we will ever do. Our gifts will come to naught without this heroic effort.

Some have asked why I don't reject all association

with Eido Shimano. I will not throw out the baby with the dirty bath water. I will never deny Eido's many strengths and gifts. In fact, one of the most important lessons he helped me realize is that one can never find Buddha in isolation from bumpkin. We are all a mix of strengths and weaknesses; just because we are weak in some areas, doesn't mean that we can't excel in others. Genki Takabayashi also taught me something that is so important to remember, that wherever we are, we are just beginning.

We all suffer from time to time from the bondage arising from the shackles of attachment, repulsion, preferences, enmeshment, idealization, vilification, righteousness, denial, self-deprecation, self-aggrandizement, self-deception and shadowy pockets of arrested development. For me, the year 2012 began with the shock that my association with ZSS and Eido Shimano had ended. Overall, I found my experience with Eido to be more beneficial than detrimental to my personal development, and thankfully I think this would be true for most (if not all) the people I encouraged to train there. Still, I had many regrets that my own appreciation of Eido, which was tinged with idealization, blinded me to the dangers of encouraging this association to others. Given my own previous blindness, I vowed that I would do all in my power to actively discourage people, especially those new to Zen, from training with Eido Shimano until his passing in 2018.

Our inner sage is a wonderful teacher, and having a teacher who can reflect and cultivate awareness of our inner sage is a gift beyond measure. The disappointment and pain that arise from recognizing the great gaps in our teachers' development can serve to enlighten us further about ourselves and the human condition. Even so, I would never wish the harm arising from my principal teachers' behaviors on anyone. Serving in the role of a teacher for decades, I can unequivocally say that my greatest regrets arise from not being a more mature well-rounded teacher. My flaws, shortcomings, gaps and mistakes have harmed others. Fortunately, I can say with confidence that my flaws and mistakes are not in the same league as those of my own principal teachers, but it may also be true that the caliber of my gifts as a teacher fall far short of theirs. When asked if I still consider myself a student of Eido Shimano I will always answer in the affirmative. I was his student and I still am, in that I'm still learning from him, as well as all the Zen ancestors. Sometimes the lessons are joyous and other times uncomfortable. The historical Buddha said take what works and leave the rest. I learned a lot from Eido about what works and as much, if not more, about what doesn't work. Even now writing this book, I'm learning more lessons from my association with him.

As I see it, when we put teachers up on pedestals, we end up diminishing ourselves and fail to protect our teachers from the harm that idealization can cause by insulating them from healthy challenges and introspection. We must be careful to realize that as human beings we will never escape our base, animalistic, bestial nature. The best we can do is become so conscious of our own base nature that we develop the skillfulness to put it in the back seat. Even with great awareness and clarity it is very difficult not to be fooled and directed by our instincts for survival that constantly try to direct us to have enough and then a little more. With time, great faith, great doubt and determination we all can come to deeper maturity, where insight rather than instinct becomes the guiding principle of our lives. Even with a great deal of true insight, we must all remain vigilant not to get tricked by *Mara* (mythological Buddhist deity of temptations) again and again.

JOURNEY WITH ROSHI JOAN HALIFAX AND ROSHI BERNIE GLASSMAN

I have learned that preparing in advance for organizational trauma is not only prudent but essential. How will an accuser be well cared for? How will the accused be well cared for? What are the structures for good care and hopefully restoration? What assurances or guidelines are put in place to assure that recommendations for redemptive steps are taken? There is no way to anticipate every possible shortcoming or conflict. Humans after all are the most complex creature on the planet and probably in a whole quadrant of the galaxy. When more than two of us get together in a group, look out! I shared an article on this subject with Shinge Roko and Roshi Joan Halifax. Both responded appreciatively. Joan has lectured about death and dying at many academic institutions and medical centers around the world. She worked with psychiatrist Stanislav Grof at the Maryland Psychiatric Research Center with dying cancer patients. She has continued to work with dying people and their families, and to teach health care professionals and family caregivers the psychosocial, ethical and spiritual aspects of care of the dying. She is also the abbot of Upaya Zen Center in Santa Fe, New Mexico.

I reached out to Roshi Joan and said that I would like to come to visit her at Upaya in the summer of 2012. She thought that was a wonderful idea and arrangements were made for me to visit in early August when I would also be able to attend a workshop by Roshi Bernie Glassman, whom I had met only briefly in 1983.

Bernie, as those who knew him called him, was born in Brooklyn, New York to Jewish immigrants in 1932. He earned an undergraduate degree in engineering from the Brooklyn Polytechnic Institute and later a Ph.D. in applied mathematics from UCLA. He first encountered Buddhism when reading *The Religions of Man* by Huston Smith, for an English class in 1958. He became a student of Taizan Maezumi Roshi and in 1967 was one of the original founding members of the Zen Center of Los Angeles (ZCLA). He was acknowledged as a Dharma Heir of Maezumi Roshi in 1995. In 1982 Bernie opened Greyston Bakery in Yonkers, New York, which first employed students training with Bernie and evolved into an organization that provided jobs for inner city residents and former convicts, many of them homeless. This went on to become the very successful Greyston Foundation. Bernie also founded the Zen Peacemakers Order, which offers many opportunities for engaged social action including homeless street retreats and Bearing Witness retreats with Native American people, and other populations, at locations such as Auschwitz-Birkenau, Rwanda, Bosnia Herzegovina, and the Holy Land.

Roshi Joan and the entire Upaya Zen Center Sangha were very welcoming and I felt warmly loved even though I had never met anyone there before. I met several times with Roshi Joan, and got to spend three fabulous days getting a good introduction to Bernie's brand of socially engaged Buddhism. I found both Roshi Joan and Bernie to be deeply liberated free spirits who have learned over the years how to bring Zen training and practice out of the "club house." I was so impressed with Bernie and his Zen Peacemakers organization that I decided then and there to attend Bernie's annual Bearing Witness Retreat at Auschwitz-Birkenau that November.

During this visit in Santa Fe, I was introduced to the Three Tenets of the Zen Peacemaker Order: 1) Not-Knowing - letting go of fixed ideas about yourself, others and the universe. In both the Zen and Quaker traditions, communing with the inconceivable is at the core of practice. 2) Bearing Witness to all the joys and sorrows and trials and tribulations of this troubled world. In meditation we learn to bear witness to all thoughts, feelings and sensations. We work to let them come and let them go with as little analysis or judgement as possible, all the while listening to the pregnant silence between and within each note of the symphony of now. 3) Taking Action that arises from communion with the inconceivable and appears to us as true insight. Taking action means courageously doing what needs doing in this moment of eternity, when action flows as naturally as water moving downhill.

Another wonderful lesson I learned from Bernie, early in our relationship, was how to make a "supreme meal." Rather than worrying about the ingredients we don't have or desire, instead, each day, make the best meal possible from the ingredients on hand. I saw Genki do this whenever he went into the kitchen, but the lesson applies not only to the kitchen but to all of life! How do we make a nutritious meal, to serve who and what's in front us this day, with only the ingredients we have? Bernie wrote a great book on this subject, *Instructions to the Cook: A Zen Master's Lessons in Living a Life That Matters*. During my visits with Roshi Joan, I felt like I had met a Dharma Aunt and I came to feel like Bernie was my Dharma Uncle. Roshi Joan counseled me to let go of my attachment to ZSS and told me it was time to move on, which at that time was a hard pill for me to swallow. Nevertheless, I was very grateful for her time and counsel.

I began having repeating nightmares of nuclear holocaust and being tortured in concentration camps shortly after my daughter was born in 1983. I came to realize that these nightmares were ascending like an eruption from my early pre-verbal abuse history. Even then in the early 1980's, I knew that one day I needed to visit one or more Nazi concentration camps because intuitively I understood there were parallels with my early torture that needed to be explored. I left for Poland on November 1, 2012, for my first Bearing Witness Retreat at Auschwitz/Birkenau and returned to Seattle on November 10.

In some ways my time in Poland visiting Auschwitz/Birkenau was exactly what I expected it to be. It was a time to sit with the deep wound in our collective unconscious arising from the Nazi effort to exterminate undesirables. Just over a hundred participants sat for five days between the sorting tracks where the trains of cattle cars dislodged thousands of people who were sorted for immediate death in the gas chambers or slave labor in the camp. Life expectancy in the camp was three months. Our meditation periods were very grounded with no distractions; it was hard to be distracted or deluded in such a place. With each inhalation all of us inhaled a small packet of the pain, loss and horror in the camp's history. Within us each small parcel of suffering was at least partially digested and then released with each exhalation. This process was repeated breath after breath, sit after sit, day after day. At the conclusion of the retreat, it felt as though the whole place was a little lighter. There is such an abundance of unprocessed suffering in this location that many more generations will be needed to release it. And so, it became my intention to return repeatedly to be with others inclined to assist with the work that needs doing.

I wasn't fully prepared for how deeply sadistic the slave labor side of the camp was. Auschwitz/Birkenau was known as a city of death, but the reality is even more horrifying. I became convinced that it was the most horrid place ever to exist on this planet. I've heard of awful things and seen many horror movies, but there is no comparison to what went on in this place. How could human beings produce this hell on earth? I've been sitting with this koan for some time now.

My first realization is that nationalism taken to its natural extreme means those not in the club become refuse. Clearly power can corrupt otherwise goodhearted people, and unlimited, unchecked power invites unspeakable cruelty. Dr. Josef Mengele is an example. He was personally responsible for unspeakable cruelties to adults and children. He was never caught and therefore never brought before a war crimes tribunal. He lived out his life hiding in Paraguay. Evidently, he claimed until his death that he had harmed no one. However, I think from his perspective he might have acknowledged that he exterminated and experimented on many cockroaches. Mengele was taught that those transported to the camp were vermin. He had a PhD in Anthropology, as well as being a medical doctor. Surely, he saw atrocities on the Eastern front where he was first posted. He saved many German soldiers' lives and became wounded himself, earning the Iron Cross. No longer able to serve at the front he was posted to Auschwitz and became the Chief

Medical Officer of the main infirmary at Birkenau.

There is no doubt in my mind that, just as with the development of cancer, there were many steps involved in Mengele's evolution from a healer to a mass murderer and one of the most heinous sadists ever known. Probably, there was a history of early abuse when Mengele was the victim. This was followed by a thorough indoctrination into racism and bigotry, rationalized as natural, appropriate and necessary throughout his school years. Additional desensitization happened when he saw horrors day after day at the Eastern Front, where members of his own tribe were being killed and maimed in front of him. And, we must not forget the reality of his own war wounds, which were severe enough that he had to be recalled from the front. Then, finally came his assignment to Auschwitz/Birkenau, where he could really erase those whom he felt were the cause of the world's problems. With this unchecked, unconditional power of life or death and the past experiences in his life, we got Dr. Mengele.

Probably all these steps were necessary to produce the cancer he became. If even one of these steps had been removed, I would likely be writing about someone else. I found myself doing prostrations at the site of Dr. Mengele's laboratory where he experimented on children, using identical twins as test subjects, infecting one and then killing both to do postmortems for "science." My prostrations were my way to apologize from my humanity to theirs for the brutality they suffered. It is also the first time I fully realized that there is not just a bumpkin but also a beast that lives in each one of us. The beast is full of fierce energy, which can be tapped and channeled appropriately for our survival or that of our kin. When this aspect is excessively oppressed it can become explosive, or if overly empowered it can become ruthless. In either of these instances this aspect can possess our higher functions and commit horrific acts against ourselves or others.

When I think of less disturbed people such as Eido Shimano and even much less disturbed characters such as Genki Takabayashi and myself, I see similar patterns. Perhaps most of us have trauma from early childhood that is carried unresolved into adulthood. I haven't met anyone who hasn't carried some baggage from childhood. In my own case, through the help of family, friends, three intense years of psychoanalysis and thirty years working through father issues with my surrogate father figures Genki Takabayashi and Eido Shimano, I have felt blessed to have made some progress. I certainly feel much less haunted by the past, and therefore, much less likely to act out my early trauma.

The best I can do in a leadership position is set the tone with my own dedication to practice. I have nothing to teach. I can only say, "look, look" or "listen to the silence" or ask core questions, which have no satisfactory conceptual answers such as, "What is this reality?" and "Who is asking?" This approach and intention keeps my role relatively simple, and also reduces the possibility of falling into the elevated guru trap that infects many spiritual leaders throughout the world.

I think it is crucial that we do not elevate spiritual guides to guru status. Those who are spiritual guides must become cognizant of the fact that early wounds and trauma can sneak up on us and have a profound impact. If we are not cognizant and appropriately cautious about this, we may begin feeding on our own communities to meet our primitive unmet needs and wants. In other words, if we are to be spiritual guides in any faith tradition, we must never feel complete and be willing to do all the inner work necessary to assure that we won't abuse our positions of trust and authority. Furthermore, it is imperative that spiritual guides seek out a close cadre of peers who aren't afraid to challenge each other.

I do have a cadre of peers locally and nationally that I consult with. I have tried to get in the habit of consulting with them early and as often as needed. Looking at my own shortcomings, I know that I get hooked when my integrity, truthfulness or motives are questioned. I do have my father's temper, but most of the time, more so with each year, I've learned to keep it in check. I've seen that the smallest error or misstep on my part is amplified exponentially by my position as a spiritual guide and a white male with vast, mostly unconscious privilege. Complicating matters further, my own early abuse history often leads me to feeling hypersensitive, fragile and prone to excessive self-disclosure. Put all this together, and still 95% of the time, I believe I live up to most people's expectations, but 5% of the time I am bound to disappoint myself and others. There is always room for improvement. We never arrive at maturity. Mastery is a process. I will always regret my errors and missteps and continue to try and learn from them.

My trip to Auschwitz certainly helped me see these sorts of situations from a deeper perspective. We are all flawed human beings with the potential to mature and grow, thereby actualizing our deep nature. In addition, we certainly have at least an equal potential to act selfishly and even sadistically from our most base instincts. Unfortunately, collectively humans are so hungry for leadership and inspiration that we have the bad habit of venerating and investing too much power in talented narcissists. How will we manage and harness our extraordinary range of potential for the benefit of all beings great and small, animate and inanimate?

On November 12, 2012 I wrote the following verse, riffing off a famous poem of Thich Nhat Hanh, "Please Call Me By My True Names":

Birkenau Reflections

A woman, tattooed with a number,
waits in the cold and rain.
Thrown out of her barracks as trash,
she is locked in a closed brick-walled courtyard.
All the gas chambers are full,
so for days she starves without food or water.
At noon perchance she hears children playing
in the nearby barracks,
knowing all too well they will soon meet the same end.

"In my opinion man,"
nationalism taken to its natural extreme means
those not in the club become refuse,
and unlimited power invites unspeakable cruelty.

I am the women curled up against the wall.

I am the child playfully drawing pictures
waiting for my mother's return.

I am the doctor who enjoys torturing the children.

I am the one angry at denial,
because I've known it all too well.

I am the one putting my head to the ground
in sorrow and shame.

I am the one meditating by the sorting tracks,
where slave labor was threshed from those to be killed,
embraced by light and rain,
chanting names of those known
and not forgetting the unknown.

Please remember to call me by my true names
so that I may be free to celebrate Shabbat
with newly found sisters and brothers calling themselves
Zen Peacemakers.

GENKI TAKABAYASHI'S BODILY DEPARTURE

On February 24, 2013 my ordination teacher died in his home in Victor, Montana. Over the course of my long association with Genki Takabayashi, I learned three profound lessons. The first thing Genki showed me about the human condition is that it is possible to transcend our likes and dislikes, preferences and opinions. During the 1980 summer *sesshin* (weeklong meditation intensive) with him, which was held at Dry Falls State Camp, the temperatures were in the nineties and the meditation hall was full of mosquitoes and flies. In addition, Mount St. Helens had a secondary eruption, flooding the air with gritty ash. To say that our meditation periods were hellish is not an understatement. During this retreat, twice a day, students would visit Genki in the *Dokusan* Room where Dharma Interviews were held. It was a small room with little ventilation, and we all concluded some animal had died and was rotting under the floorboards. In the meditation hall and Dokusan Room, Genki sat serenely unmoving in full-lotus, with a beneficent countenance, seemingly impervious to adversity. Genki often related that as a young man at his first Daitoku-Ji sesshin in Japan, after three days he thought he would die from pain and exhaustion, and hoped there would be an earthquake to bring the roof down to end his suffering. Yet, by the conclusion of the seven-day retreat there had been a shift where he became confident that if an earthquake brought the roof down that somehow, he would remain seated amid the rubble.

The second gift I received from Genki was the opportunity to soak up his actualization that an "enlightened" life is an "ordinary" life. In everything he approached he demonstrated that living life fully with "everyday openhearted activity" was paramount. No matter if it was sitting zazen, cooking, calligraphy, gardening, landscaping, cleaning, pottery, giving Teisho, making a bowl of whisked green tea or writing fiction, Genki was fully present to the activity at hand, operating with joy, unending enthusiasm and energy. He taught us that *samu* (work meditation) was more important to our training than zazen, sutra recitation or koan study.

The third lesson learned, the hardest to accept and perhaps the most important, is that all of us are fully human. Even though Genki amply demonstrated that we can be and are all vessels of the Dharma, we are also limited, and from time to time stubbornly primitive. There will always be tension between our base instincts and true insight. When Genki left Japan, he abandoned a relationship and a child. He never understood credit or money well and often found himself in debt. Early on during his time in Seattle we had to warn female participants that there was a good chance he would make a pass at them. Only more recently have I learned of the many women he harmed by his inappropriate pursuits and affairs. As I learned from Eido Shimano, we are all a blend of Buddha and bumpkin, but as I have come to understand, I think it is more accurate to say we are all a blend of Buddha and Beast. Moreover, with all the training in the world we will never arrive at completion or full enlightenment. In my view, there is no such thing as complete enlightenment. I often tell the story of how, at least once a year, Genki would give a Teisho where he would exclaim, "I now just beginning to understand, just now beginning to see."

Everyone has limitations and shortcomings that arise from wounds in our history. There are three options for dealing with them. One is to do the very difficult work of combusting, digesting and integrating these wounds. Or, we can try to contain them so that they don't cause harm to others. Finally, we can skip over them with spiritual bypassing, which can be easily done; usually though, they come back to haunt us. Like most of us, Genki made use of all three.

Genki proved time and again that he could be an inspirational catalyst for those training with him. He probed and prompted the Chobo-Ji Sangha to investigate and experience the depth of our true nature, a bottomless vastness without form that gives rise to everything. He taught mainly by example how to live fully and passionately, with an attentive caring attitude, beyond any attachment to rank, position, preference or opinion. He became a surrogate father to me, and I will always be grateful for his continuing presence in my life.

JOURNEY WITH JOAN AND BERNIE CONTINUES

Thoughts about my upcoming second trip to Auschwitz/Birkenau occupied me during part of Chobo-Ji's annual weeklong Autumn meditation retreat in 2013. I examined more deeply the truth that each of us is a mix of Buddha and Hitler. No one can ever be Buddha nor Hitler in isolation. Reality is a big soup where these ingredients can't be isolated from each other. Even to speak of Buddha or Hitler as opposites demonstrates our lack of understanding and reveals that we are already stuck in concepts. Before deep awakening, we talk about being Buddha and Hitler as being separate and different, after deep awakening we see clearly there's no Buddha and no Hitler, there's just THIS. Occasionally, people get lopsided and lean heavily into the Buddha side of their nature or the Hitler side of their nature.

Maturity is realizing the truth that we include all these different polarities all wrapped up in one package. Given this truth, where does that leave us? This can be explored in the meditation hall with contemplative prayer; however, deep testing can only happen in our daily life with our neighbors. The meditation hall or Quaker Meeting House are great laboratories to investigate these polarities, and to explore our deep nature beyond these polarities. We are attracted to this deep exploration because we realize this life is but a brief blip. In meditation we can explore the whole spectrum of reality, but if our exploration is limited to the meditation hall, church or temple all our practice and training will fail at being truly useful. Unless we're able to bring our integration out into the wider world, our practice will fall far short of real maturity. The best testing is done while engaged in acts of service. Being of service to Mother Earth, caring for creatures great and small, animate and inanimate is where the rubber meets the road.

Without testing and expanding of our practice into the wider world, deep religious or spiritual training can implode. Unfortunately, as I have learned, anything can be corrupted and the highest teaching can be brought low. Vigilance helps us to not be fooled by smoke and mirrors. Although the light, ritual and form may draw us into spiritual practice and introduce us to great clarity, peacefulness and a loving heart, these experiences will be of limited value if we are not able to share it with our families and in our vocations. I have great gratitude towards my spiritual practices in Zen and Quaker meeting, but I must remember to not get fooled! Practice in the temple or Quaker Meeting House is only the beginning of training.

I have no doubt that on occasion Hitler was a nice guy. And no doubt the real, historical Buddha sometimes got up on the wrong side of the bed. We must learn to accept, balance and integrate our various polarities in ways that benefit each other and Mother Earth.

At the end of my second Bearing Witness Retreat to Auschwitz/Birkenau I wrote the following reflection verse:

Hell on Earth, no words can properly convey.
Millions of men, women and children
  reduced to objects,
toys to be sadistically played with,
refuse to be burnt and discarded.

At first no one could believe such horrific events
  were possible in the 20th century.
Who could have guessed genocide would
  continue almost unabated?
Have we learned nothing from the past?
How many more centuries or millennium
  will it take before humankind more fully
  realizes that we are all one body, one soul.

A man sees his parents, his wife, his sisters, his
  children take the path to the left.
Only the smell of burning flesh and smoke from
  the chimneys remains.

This same man finds the courage not to be slave
labor for those who have taken his loved ones.
Full of determination and repose he walks into
     the electric fence.

Decades later the grass is green,
a rabbit scurries between barracks,
a rainbow arches over the camp,
Peacemakers remember
     with meditation and song,
among them two find love
     and courageously marry.

Elie Wiesel writes upon receiving the Nobel Peace
prize: "We must take sides. Neutrality helps the
oppressor, never the victim. Silence encourages the
tormentor, never the tormented. Sometimes we
must interfere. When human lives are endangered,
when human dignity is in jeopardy, national
borders and sensitivities become irrelevant...."

Both the Jewish people and the Palestinian people
have lost too many sons and daughters and
shed too much blood. This must stop, and all
attempts to stop it must be encouraged. Israel will
cooperate I am sure of that. I trust Israel."
I for one do not. I have no solution,
but I am confident that

when the conflict concludes, and it will,
it will be because peacemakers dared to trust
where nations would not.

Who sees the golden sunset
through the fences of Birkenau?
White tailed deer bound down
the old path of death.

Deep within all of us is a kind of crazy core. When contained properly, it can be like a furnace that generates warmth and energy. When not properly contained, it will destroy anyone who is not considered to be in our tribe. If really let loose, it may even kill our family and us. This inner core when uncontained is quite crazy. It is the seed of our corporeal body's instincts for survival. It gives rise to the separate sense of selfhood. And our selfhood, or ego identity, seeks protection - and it needs protection! The first ring of our social group is our family, and we identify with family and need to protect family. But these needs for protection, safety, having enough, and then maybe a little more, when unchecked by something broader and deeper, leads to what is known as "exponential suffering" and symptoms such as greed, and even a murderous rage to protect and grab territory. We may be expelled or even killed if we are found trespassing in the territory claimed by another's crazy core. In meditation it is easy to recognize this grasping, attaching, judging, discriminating, worrying, fearful mind. We probably all know what it's like to be possessed by our fearful mind. When our crazy core of survival instincts possesses us, we're very unhappy, we can never have enough; we all become hungry ghosts. It's hopeful that during the process of meditation we learn how to recognize the grasping mind and peacefully say: "Let go and let be" or "Let go, and let God." With this mantra we can drop into something much broader and deeper. This practice gives us a sense of being grounded and connected to something vast and boundless. Awareness of this connection fosters equanimity and clarity. Indeed, when we get up from meditation, we feel clear about what needs doing and have the peace of mind and energy to do it.

I work diligently to be as truthful, clear, sincere and openhearted as I possibly can. This is especially true in my work as a psychotherapist and spiritual guide. In these roles it's exceedingly important that I be able to genuinely embody equanimity, clarity and loving support. Of course, I don't always succeed in this. In addition, I'm aware of my basic primitive nature that grabs me from time to time. To the extent that I'm a good therapist, spiritual guide and parent, I'm able to protect others from being affected by the primitive crazy core that resides within me.

One of the worst things that could be said of a spiritual guide, therapist or a parent is that they took advantage of their position of authority for their own selfish use or gain. Occasionally I wear the purple *kesa* (symbolic robe of the historical Buddha) given to me by Eido Shimano, and it's full of his Zen-sweat. Why do I continue to wear this robe? With many followers of the Way, including myself, he held the relationship boundaries well. He held the container of practice for me in such a way that together we could awaken ever more deeply to our original nature, which is immensely vaster than our crazy core. For this I'm full of gratitude. On the other hand, an e-book written by Mark Oppenheimer, *The Zen-Predator of the Upper East Side*, published by The Atlantic Books, was released in December, 2013. That's my core-teacher Eido Shimano, who served me well, but preyed on many female students to serve his own sexual appetite and addiction. Shinge Roko called Oppenheimer's book a "lurid pursuit of sexual titillation." The book is far from perfect or complete, but it is the best collection I've seen to date that gives an adequate overview of Eido Shimano's deplorable behavior over many decades.

Genki Takabayashi, Eido Shimano, Joshu Sasaki, Taizan Maezumi, among other Zen leaders, have revealed for all of us to see that they are flawed, psychologically damaged human beings. And each one has also demonstrated that they are vessels of the Dharma/Light/ Truth. I too am a psychologically damaged human being. Yet, this doesn't prevent me or anyone from being a vessel of the Dharma. Maturity, aided by acceptance, humility, service and practice, takes time! With practice and time, we can ripen and prepare ourselves, as best we can, to be in ordinary life with more maturity. Each period of meditation or contemplative prayer allows us to march on. We can become skillful at connecting to our own deep nature, and this effort will help us mature beyond our species adolescence. My wish is for everyone to contribute to this flowering of mature human potential.

Before this flowering can take place, we must come to the realization individually and collectively that we all are really extensions of one body, soul and mind. We must more fully realize that our separate identities are a delusion; each of us is unique, but none of us are separate from each other. During my second trip to Auschwitz/Birkenau, I found myself during the fourth day of the Bearing Witness Retreat, lying down in a bunk located in a small barracks that housed perhaps a hundred men or more. Four or five people would be put side by side in one flat bunk, three bunks stacked on top of each other, as in a slave-ship. As I lay down in the dust, I felt an instant horror. What was it like to be a slave laborer in this barracks?

The men who were more fit were separated from most women, children and old people. Likely these men saw their parents, children and wives take the path to the left, which led immediately to the gas chambers. Soon they realized that the only reason they were kept alive was to serve the Third Reich as slave labor. I got so acutely depressed, lying in that bunk that I couldn't speak. The dark depression did not begin to lift until I realized what I would have to do if I found myself in their position. For me it would have been the right decision to walk, with determination and repose into the electric fence, rather than be used and abused further in the service to the Third Reich. Seven decades after the camp was closed, it was abundantly clear one way or another I would have never survived this city of death.

During this visit the grass was green, a rabbit scurried between barracks and a beautiful rainbow fell over the center of the camp. Peacemakers sat in meditation between the sorting tracks. I sat with one hundred people from all over the world. As we sat, we remembered those fallen by calling out names. One day all the women peacemakers gathered in one of the women's barracks; likewise, men gathered in a men's barrack. The barracks where the women gathered was the last stop for women fully exhausted and waiting to die. All the labor had been squeezed out of them. There was no reason to feed the women brought there because they could not offer any further service to the Third Reich. The gas chambers were reserved for the thousands just coming off the transport trains, so the women in this barracks often died of starvation. If no bunk was available women were forced to sleep outside in the wet and cold. Visiting such a place decades later, something of their depression can soak into you.

Collectively we must wake up. We may not realize how easy it is for any of us to be possessed by the primitive beast within. When seriously possessed we become capable of abusing or killing our own children. We must wake up and grow up. Can we do it? I believe we can, but to do so we need to learn how not to be directed and controlled by our personal instincts of survival. We can learn to use our inner fire for good purposes. It can be done.

On our last day in the camp in November of 2013, there was a golden sunset, shining through the trees, barbed wire and the guard towers. All of us were preparing to leave the camp, and a white-tailed deer bounded down the old isles of death. Exiting the camp from the pool that was full of ashes from the crematoriums, we walked the same path of death with the white-tailed deer in the golden sunset.

We can cultivate our compassion; we don't have to be directed by our inner beast. Yet, the fact is that we are all disabled in some ways, physically, psychologically or spiritually. This guarantees that no corporeal form can always be a perfect vessel of the Dharma or Holy Spirit. On the other hand, no matter how corrupted, confused and deluded we are, even mass murderers are also vessels of the Dharma!

In March, 2014, Bernie traveled to Seattle to be part of a daylong workshop on "Living a Life that Matters." About 200 people were in attendance. The day before the workshop, I picked Bernie up at the airport when he arrived in Seattle and was delighted to share some private time with him walking around nearby Jefferson Park. I felt so very grateful for our deepening association and for the organization he founded, Zen Peacemakers.

On the last day of Chobo-Ji's 2014 Spring Sesshin I ordained as a Zen novice priest (unsui) Mark Rinzan Pechovnik. When I met Rinzan a couple of years earlier, I assumed he was already an unsui. He had trained many years at Great Vow Monastery, and carried himself in a way that makes all that training obvious. He had already done more than 30 weeklong sesshins. For me to consider someone for ordination they must be willing to dedicate their life to the propagation of Zen Buddhist practice for the benefit of all beings, do a minimum of four consecutive sesshins at Chobo-Ji following the taking of the Buddhist Precepts and be willing to do four sesshins a year, at least until the count of 40 sesshins is reached. Rinzan had exceeded these requirements and made a deep commitment to his vows. Rinzan would go on to become Osho (temple priest) and then my first Dharma Heir and currently runs the No-Rank Zendo in Portland Oregon. I feel blessed to be associated with him and we have become deep friends.

In mid-April of 2014, Carolyn and I traveled with 28 others from around the globe to the East Africa city of Kigali in Rwanda. We were there to join with 30 East Africans for a weeklong Bearing Witness Retreat around the aftermath of the 100 days of genocide that took place there in 1994 where nearly a million people were slaughtered. Originally there was little to no animosity between the two main tribes inhabiting what would become Rwanda, but beginning with German and then Belgian colonialization and interference, tensions were fostered between the main two tribes, Tutsis and Hutus. This tension eventually erupted as a series of civil wars and multiple genocides between the tribes. Visiting Rwanda was a transformative occasion for me. As with all the Bearing Witness Retreats I've attended, the Zen Peacemakers, founded by Roshi Bernie Glassman, ran the retreat.

This was the third five-day Bearing Witness Retreat I had attended with Bernie, his wife Eve, and many talented well-trained support staff. As I have related, Bernie had been holding retreats in Auschwitz for over twenty years. People from all over the world have attended these retreats. The format of a Bearing Witness retreat is to face the horrors that have happened in a location, through eyewitness testimony whenever possible, by visiting memorial museums, and most directly by sitting in meditation for at least four hours a day at the site of the atrocities. In Rwanda, we did meditation next to a mass grave where 50,000 men, women and children were killed in the course of seven hours in a place called Murambi.

In the morning and evenings Council was held where we processed in a group what we had witnessed. The morning Council was a small group of eight people, at the evening Council the whole group gathered. The rules for the Council are: 1) Speak from the Heart, perhaps a concern, doubt, joy, sorrow, or whatever feels most real, 2) Listen from the Heart with empathy for the speaker, hearing various viewpoints of one Mind, 3) Speak Spontaneously (no planned remarks, what's come forth in this council), 4) Speak Leanly (no fat, no back story, considerate of others), 5) Confidentiality, share nothing outside of council that might identify a speaker other than yourself. This process went on during each of our days together.

In Rwanda, my small group included a rehabilitated perpetrator who had killed many during the genocide. He told how he first refused to kill his neighbors, but then was shot in the leg for not doing so. After that, the next time he was told to kill, he did so. A young woman in our group who survived the genocide when she was a babe in arms become so distraught hearing the perpetrator's account that she broke down sobbing and had to leave our small group and join another. One woman, who had her baby cut in two, her hand cut off at her wrist and was left to die in a swamp, was also in attendance. The same man, who became a perpetrator, acknowledged that he had been the one to cut off this woman's hand. The two had reconciled through the national reconciliation and redemption process called Gacaca. When the retreat concluded these two got off at the same bus stop together and, standing next to each other, waved goodbye to the rest of us. There was an awkward but real peace between them.

At night we stayed at a church conference center about a mile from the Murambi memorial site. Each morning and evening, most of us walked the steep mile along a narrow, non-paved, heavily rutted road through a small village to the memorial site. Some of the people we passed were curious, others skeptical, some perhaps astonished, but most seemed happy and honored that we were there to bear witness and reached out to hold our hands, as if to say, "Thank you for coming and being a witness to this horror even twenty years later. We very much appreciate your efforts to honor our dead."

As a person of faith, I am devoted to seeing everyone as a blossoming Buddha/Christ, and everything as a manifestation of Nature. It is sometimes hard to reconcile these intentions with the fact that we are the only creature on the planet that can slaughter a whole group of people because they don't belong to "our" group. Perhaps activating this deeply seated potential to dehumanize our fellow beings and cruelly massacre them in the most cruel and sadistic way has had some survival value in our ancient past. In any case, if we fail to recognize and accept that we all have this potential to sink into a murderous mob hysteria, we are bound to globally repeat this awful pattern indefinitely.

Perhaps our species will prove itself to be an evolutionary dead-end, a non-viable Voice of the Truth and Spirit. Will our species outgrow our collective adolescence? Do we have the capacity to learn difficult truths about ourselves before it is too late? Fortunately, often out of great suffering come waves of awareness and seeds of deep compassion. This is very evident in Rwanda, 20 years after the genocide, where they say, "Iyo Umenya Nawe Ukimenya Ntuba Waranyishe" (If you knew who I am, and you knew who you are, you wouldn't have killed me).

Here is the verse I wrote on the last night of the Rwanda retreat, April 19, 2014...

Africa Reflections:
Investigating the Inconceivable

Who maims, kills, rapes and tortures others?

Who can bash the heads of children
against a brick wall?

The tropical rains wash away the blood
but not the stains.

Within us must lie a beast that feeds on fear and hate.
How did it get there?
Has it been inside from the beginning?
What purpose does it serve?
Seen or unseen Mars shines brightly overhead.

Like a dormant virus the beast waits for opportunity.
When it takes hold, ANYONE can become violent.

In a pandemic, genocide can sweep like fire.
The fire may ignite a nation, a region or the world.
The 50,000 dead of Murambi do not lie.

How do we keep the virus in check?
Rwanda shows the way.
First put out the fire.
Don't seek revenge.

Offer a path for redemption and reconciliation.
Study our nature.
No denial of the past.
No denial of our potential for good or evil.
Above all strengthen love and understanding.

There is so much we cannot know.

Who are we really?

Hawks and doves circle together over a thousand fertile hills.

Speaking from the heart reveals there is no "other."

Shu Jo Mu Hen Sei Gan Do
(We vow to care for all.)

For me joining a Bearing Witness retreat is one way that I can personally actualize my intention to care for all beings. Here in Seattle, I participate actively in the state wide Faith Action Network (FAN – fanwa.org), which gathers religious leaders and people of faith around workable social action goals. With this group, I have talked repeatedly to Governor Inslee about halting the death penalty in Washington state through an executive order putting a moratorium on all executions. Among many other issues, FAN actively works on gun control legislation, police accountability, housing and Native American issues.

Rwanda changed me. Oddly, I'm somehow happier knowing that I too could have been converted into a serial murderer! The range of the human condition runs from cruel sadistic predator to beneficent sage. If we don't realize that this whole spectrum is our real nature then we are living with blinders on. Knowing more concretely the reality of our nature puts a lot of things in perspective. With this perspective it is easier to relax into this life and death journey with a caring heart.

Being a Zen Master is not as simple as decades of training, a few breakthroughs and writing some verse. Zen training never helps us attain anything because our deep nature is already with us and can never leave. Our deep nature is already revealed in every thought and action. Nevertheless, perhaps in the course of a contemplative silent retreat, we can from time to time leap forward beyond our superficial right or wrong thinking, beyond attachment to young or old, male or female, beyond our likes and dislikes. Practice is not about enlightenment. It is about learning how to cut our attachments and repulsions that hide our light. As we get more skillful at combusting and breaking through, we are bound to mature a bit, and this is undoubtedly helpful to everyone we encounter.

As a white male in a leadership role, and most of the Chobo-Ji Sangha also being white, I realize it is difficult for people of color to find a home in this Sangha. Moreover, in general I think it is fair to say that Rinzai Zen tends to attract more males than females, and given how women have been preyed upon by so many male Zen teachers, it is no wonder that women are particularly cautious about this practice. I'm not at all surprised that many women find it more comfortable to train with a woman Zen teacher. Even though the Chobo-Ji Sangha is working hard to understand the imbedded structural racism and patriarchy in every institution and organization, people of color may well need to train with a teacher or community that has gained greater sensitivity and awareness then I or the Chobo-Ji Sangha can yet offer. As a white male with lots of intrinsic privilege, some of which is difficult for me to see, it is harder for me to understand the natural doubts, fears, anger and sensitivities of women and people of color. At least I'm aware of this, and working hard to explore the blind spots that go along with white male privilege and fragility. I work to have more tolerance and less reactivity to the transference that is bound to come my way as a white male in a leadership position. All this, is of course, much easier said than done.

We all carry a portion of karmic baggage handed to us from our family of origin, cultural programing and national history. Unfortunately, even late in life, much of this baggage can remain unconscious. Nevertheless, I remain convinced that with dedicated spiritual practice, and the readiness of time, much of our karmic baggage and cultural programing becomes self-evident. This is when the hard work begins. It takes a long time to compost this baggage. If we can stay with the practice and face our shadow without doing spiritual bypassing, then the compost becomes great fertilizer. To cultivate this kind of patience, every spiritual community must work at being a welcoming place of sincere, kind practice. Unquestionably, we all have a lot of work to do. If we think we have arrived, we are fooling ourselves. Undoubtedly, there will be some missteps, blowups and blowouts along the way. Nevertheless, we've got to stick to the practices that break down all artificial barriers because we are all a part of one fabric. Even with sincere and dedicated practice, unprocessed karmic knots will be passed on to the next generation. We can't get through all the knots in one generation, but it is incumbent on each generation to untangle as much as we can. My Zen Dharma great-grandfather is Yamamoto Gempo Roshi. He was famous for saying that the real purpose of meditation is not awakening or spiritual union (which is relatively easy) but is for creating the spaciousness, awareness and heat (fire of determination) needed to combust our stuck generational baggage – *Shuku-go* (dried karmic dung wedged in one's gut).

The next Bearing Witness Retreat I did with Bernie was held in the Black Hills of South Dakota, hosted by the Lakota peoples and facilitated by Zen Peacemaker organizers. Before my departure for South Dakota, Monika Jion Winkelmann, a Zen student from Germany visiting

Seattle, made connections with Seattle's Duwamish tribal members (the local tribe that long lived by the nearby Duwamish river). On July 27, 2015, six Chobo-Ji Sangha members traveled the short distance from our temple to the Duwamish Longhouse to chant the Heart Sutra for the tribe and deliver a ritual pouch of tobacco from our temple to tribal member Ken Workman. Ken in turn gave us a pouch of tobacco from the tribe to travel with us as an offering gift to the Lakota peoples. Chobo-Ji also handed Ken a scroll authored by Monika and me to the tribe, which said, "With expression of deep sorrow and broken hears, with feelings of regret and honor that the people occupying this region and nation have not better listened and cared for the sorrows inflicted on the indigenous population and their descendants. I and other members of Chobo-Ji fully support your continued efforts for recognition and redress of the wrongs that have been done, to assure that the Duwamish people are always here and respected in their homeland." The tribe framed our scroll and it now hangs in the Duwamish Longhouse. Chobo-Ji and many Chobo-Ji Sangha members support the tribe each month with a donation to Real Rent Duwamish. Moreover, I have become an ally and advocate for the Duwamish tribe at the city, regional and national levels of government. The tribe is still fighting for legal recognition in the federal courts. Many tribal members never moved to a reservation and still live in the city which takes its name from Chief Si'ahl (Seattle).

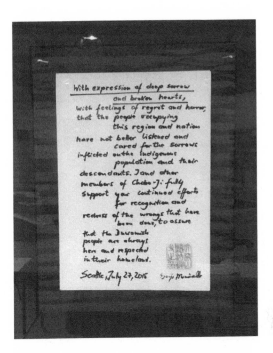

With expression of deep sorrow
and broken hearts,
with feelings of regret and horror,
that the people occupying
this region and nation
have not better listened and
cared for the sorrows
inflicted on the Indigenous
population and their
descendants. I and other
members of Chobo-Ji fully
support your continued efforts
for recognition and
redress of the wrongs that have
been done, to assure
that the Indigenous
people are always
here and respected
in their homeland.

Seattle, July 29, 2015   Genjo Marinello

The Native American Bearing Witness Retreat was held from August 10-14, 2015. This retreat took more than five years to organize – primarily to build mutual trust. The Lakota peoples hosted the retreat on land bought by them in the heart of the Black Hills; it is ironic and tragic that the tribes had to purchase a parcel of land in the middle of territory that the United States Supreme Court has conceded was illegally taken from them. The tribes have refused the price the federal government has offered as recompense for the land and are still awaiting either the return of the lands or, at least, control of the land's care and its resources.

At the retreat, each morning started with a ceremony of all 200 participants standing in a huge circle around a perpetual campfire. During the ceremony respect and acknowledgement was given to the seven directions honoring all relatives. The sharing and talks moved me deeply. Three memories particularly stand out. One memory is of Steven Newcomb, who helped us understand the deep racism imbedded in the Doctrine of Christian Discovery which was used and is still referenced by courts as the legal foundation for claiming and confiscating all non-Christian lands and subjugating, displacing, and (in the past) enslaving and eliminating native peoples and their cultures. Steven wrote a book, *Pagan in the Promised Land*, that has moved me greatly.

The second memory is of a talk given by Charmaine White Face, a mother, grandmother, great-grandmother, spokesperson for the Sioux Nation Treaty Council, and author of the book, *Indigenous Nations Rights*. Ms. White Face founded Defenders of the Black Hills and helped found Clean Up the Mines (both organizations exist to better the life of the Lakota peoples). She gratefully received the pouch that Jion and I transported from the Duwamish peoples, promising to honor it on her altar. Perhaps the most intense encounter of our days together was listening to and sitting with the late Beatrice Long Visitor Holy Dance, an Oglala Lakota elder from the Pine Ridge Reservation, best known for her participation in the International Council of 13 Indigenous Grandmothers. At the time she was in her nineties and had traveled around the world in support of indigenous peoples. While we were together at this retreat, we heard of at least two suicides of young natives. I asked her how she dealt with the fact that so many native sons and daughters were killing themselves. She said, "Our young people are so distraught, lost, confused and unrooted because their culture has been decimated and the poverty is so oppressive that they hurry their return to Mother Earth in any way that they can. From their viewpoint they have no other way to return or feel connected." I know everyone present was very moved by this wise and compassionate perspective.

The Oglala Lakota County, where most of the Pine Ridge Reservation is located, is the poorest county in all 50 states. The annual per capita income today is less than $9,000. This county also has the highest suicide rate in the nation. Many people live in poorly insulated trailer homes, often three generations reside in a single home. Every Indian treaty made has been broken. Year after year lands have been confiscated or leased to white ranchers. Before Indian casinos were opened, every chance to excel and achieve some measure of independence on the bad lands that remained to them was crushed. For a long time, reservations were like prisoner-of-war camps managed by the Department of Defense. On reservations native languages and cultural rituals were forbidden. Native people were denied citizenship and therefore voting rights. Children were forcibly taken from their families and lodged in boarding schools. These times were within the memory of native elders at the conference. All of this and much more is documented well in a book I have recently read and highly recommend, *The Inconvenient Indian: A Curious Account of Native People in North America* by Thomas King.

Despite this horrendous history the native presenters exhibited great dignity and resilience and had a lot to offer the non-native participants in attendance from around the world. For example, we were told a myth by a park ranger of native descent. It was a story about a recent gathering of winged and four-legged peoples who congregated at the heart of Turtle Island. At this gathering an assessment was made of the two-legged peoples who now inhabited this territory. Rather than revealing the assessment of the winged and four-legged peoples, the park ranger asked the white people in his audience the following turning question, "What do you think their assessment would be?" and let the story hang in the silence that followed.

The native elders at the retreat told us how the tribes through generations of loss and oppression nearly lost their connection to Mother Earth, and reminded us, so have we all. We were told repeatedly by many native speakers that, "Our Mother misses us." I know this to be true in my bones. Long before ever preparing for this trip to the Black Hills, I often said that meditation is one way we can help ourselves remember that we are earthlings. We do this by planting our tailbone deep into the vast, dark, fertile, nurturing, cleansing intimacy of Mother Earth. The meditation hall is a laboratory for reestablishing a conscious communion with Mother Earth.

At another sharing we heard a Native American linguist who was asked (as part of her graduate studies) to translate a Lakota document that was written about one hundred years ago. This was a time when native cohesion and culture were collapsing from the constant pressure of the ever-expanding needs of white settlers which forced the tribes into shrinking reservations. In this document, which was the transcription of a native elder of that time, the elder gave his impression of the wave of principally European settlers occupying his homeland. He said, "this second wave of people to this land, appear to have no idea about truth or honesty. They don't know how to keep their word. They don't know how be on the land without exhausting all resources in their path. They know nothing about harmonizing with nature. They know nothing about how to care for the land or even each other. How can they last? With their numbers and violence, now is their time, but it will necessarily be short because they rape the land and don't know how to care for others. One hundred years from now the Lakota peoples will surely have another turn, because this new culture can't possibly survive."

At this Bearing Witness retreat any native from any part of the country could attend at no cost on a full scholarship. Because of crushing poverty, most natives would not be able to find alternatives for taking care of their children and elders; moreover, most of those with jobs would not be able to afford the time away from work. These limitations meant that paying Europeans and white occupiers substantially outnumbered the Native American attendees. Another reason it was difficult to attract native attendees was the skepticism held by First Peoples believing that non-natives would not be able to honestly look at the collective harm done historically and currently to natives and their culture. Could non-natives look in the mirror and see their collusion in generations of tragedy? From the native perspective was it worth risking trust one more time? Would this retreat lead to any kind of shift in consciousness appropriate to sharing their soul? Despite this doubt, mistrust and abundant appropriate caution, many people from the First Nations did attend. And they did risk sharing their stories, truths, hardships and spirituality with non-native friends. I feel so fortunate to have had the opportunity to listen and learn.

On the last night of the retreat, we all gathered in one final circle, for a peace-pipe ceremony. The pipe went around the circle once with a smoke blessing; the second time around each of the 200 people was offered a chance to share something from their heart-mind. I think everyone could sense that in that circle we all expressed some facet of the collective heart-mind of humanity. We all left feeling we had been heard. In addition, we all left with a good measure of determination to go forth and soothe and perhaps heal the rifts between peoples. I felt very depressed by the sorrows shared and at the same time enlivened by the grounded, resilient, welcoming efforts of those hosting this retreat. It remains amazing to me that cultures that have been so brutally oppressed can still be rich and vibrant after suffering numerous atrocities and having access to only minimal resources. The two-legged peoples are, after all, of one family, and we must collectively come to embrace this more deeply in order stop raping our planet and ourselves. Are we ready to die for Mother Earth? She has given and is giving us so much. I'm happy to say that I learned later that many people at this conference, both native and colonizers, became water protectors. The Earth *is* crying for us to come home.

The Black Hills retreat was my fourth Bearing Witness Retreat in four years. At this point in my relationship with Bernie it was my intention to do one Bearing Witness Retreat a year; however, in 2016 I made a trip to India instead. In 2017 my mother was dying, so I didn't go then. In 2018 I returned to Auschwitz/Birkenau. Unfortunately, Bernie did not attend this Bearing Witness Retreat, as he was ill. It was the first time he had ever missed one. Sadly, we got the news while we were in retreat that he had passed on. I have not been to a Bearing Witness retreat since he died, but I'm sure I will go again one day. I am saying all this now because I had no idea that August, 2015 would be the last time that I would be with him in bodily form. Nevertheless, I always feel him with me.

JOURNEY TO INDIA WITH HOZAN ALAN SENAUKE

On the last full day of Chobo-Ji's Autumn weeklong sesshin in 2016, many Sangha members, including myself, helped move heavy bags of dirt to the yard-waste dump truck. Unfortunately, I think this action along with doing my usual full lotus for a week, caused what I thought was my right hip to go out of alignment. On the last morning of this retreat, I found it impossible to go downstairs from my apartment to the meditation hall!

After several osteopathic treatments, my right leg began to work again. However, I was left with so much numbness in my right foot and weakness in my right leg that it produced a substantial limp. I started weekly physical therapy and saw a rehabilitation doctor, who recommended that I see a surgeon. Through this injury I've gained more empathy for everyone who is disabled in some way. I especially gained empathy for my daughter who has a genetically inherited progressive nerve disorder that slows signals from her extremities and makes it hard for her to walk.

Shortly after Autumn Sesshin and before seeing a surgeon, I left for a great adventure in India. I had never been that far away from Seattle before. I can honestly say I had never wanted to go to India and I had always wanted to go to India. I never wanted to go because I thought the injustice and disparities ingrained in the caste system would overwhelm my ability to bear witness. I worried that I would either collapse in despair or become too callous to care. On another level it was just this challenge to bear witness that called me to the country. Moreover, I felt called to pilgrimage to the sites frequented by the historical Buddha, such as Vulture Peak where he gave many discourses, the Bodhi Tree under which he sat when he awoke to Buddha Nature, and Sarnath where he gave his first sermon on the Four Noble Truths to five ascetics.

Hozan Alan Senauke, whom I have long admired and with whom I enjoyed spending time at Upaya, invited me to attend a conference sponsored by the International Network of Engaged Buddhists and the Nagaloka Buddhist Training Center in Nagpur, India. Hozan is a Soto Zen priest, folk musician, poet, recently installed abbot of Berkeley Zen Center, former Executive Director of the Buddhist Peace Fellowship and head of the Clear View Project. It has taken some time to process this visit and digest what I saw and heard. Perhaps I will never fully integrate this one visit to India. I hope to go again someday. With its long history, diverse peoples and extreme contrasts, I doubt anyone really knows India.

My journey to India began with a flight from Seattle to Paris on October 8, 2016; there I transferred to a flight to Mumbai. When I arrived in Mumbai, my one checked bag did not. I spent the night in Mumbai and took a flight to Nagpur the next morning. I only saw my bag again when I returned to Mumbai the evening of October 18 for my flight back to Paris. The Mumbai airport is the most opulent airport I have ever visited. It is immaculate and futuristic – a kind of national museum of Indian culture and art. Outside the airport in the busy streets, one is assailed by an intense cacophony of sights, sounds and smells, and a boiling mix of rich and poor. Nearby is a cramped ghetto of shacks where thousands of people live and work under a sea of blue tarps.

Since I only had the clothes on my back for the whole time I was in the sub-continent, I hand washed my underwear each night and by morning they were dry. In a small way this minor hardship brought me a bit closer to the poverty of many that I met. Most of the students who attend Nagaloka come from the Dalit (untouchable) caste, and never felt truly human before setting foot on the campus. Just the fact that Buddhists from all over the world would be willing to accept and drink from a glass of tea handed from them was miraculous and transformative. The students could feel our genuine thanks and respect. Two insights stand out. One, just how radical the idea of Sangha was in the time of the historical Buddha; to accept women and anyone from any caste was revolutionary. He proclaimed that even female Dalits' lives mattered and they could join the Sangha. Second, that we too have a caste system here in the United States. It is not as pervasive and ancient as in India, but very real, with Native Americans and Blacks at the bottom of the heap. At the conference, Hozan gave a visionary talk, "Breaking Down Barriers Between People."

Hozan began his talk speaking about India's visionary constitution, which was confirmed by India's new parliament towards the end of January, 1950. One of its principal authors was Dr. B. R. Ambedkar, who was a Dalit himself and suffered horrible discrimination, but managed to get a series of postgraduate degrees from Columbia University and the London School of Economics.

Dr. Ambedkar was a jurist, economist, politician and most of all a social reformer who worked tirelessly to mitigate social discrimination towards the Dalits. Later in life he converted to Buddhism and initiated a movement of mass conversions of the Dalits. The Indian constitution parallels the teachings of the Buddha and both recognize the fundamental delusion of humanity to separate self from other, us from them. Together the tracks of secular governance and spiritual liberation can work to reflect our seamless interdependence with all beings. Realizing our seamlessness and interdependence inspires us to work for equality and justice for all members of society. The secular constitution of India was written to align with the fundamentally anti-racist spiritual doctrine of Buddhism. Nevertheless, across India, despite many constitutional protections, terrible caste and gender-based atrocities are reported daily. Of course, in most places around the world and certainly in the United States there are similar disparities and atrocities.

Hozan concluded his talk by reminding his listeners that the barriers we grew up with that separate others into race or caste do not simply disappear with the realization that these artificial barriers are false. They continue to exist in our minds long after this realization and continue to corrupt us and society. Hozan says, "Each of us must do the work as if the whole world's suffering is our responsibility. Because it is. The Dhamma [Dharma] provides the tools by which we chip away at barriers — those within ourselves and those between us. But remember: we must rely on each other. We are never alone. Nothing stands between us."

At the Nagaloka Buddhist Training Center in Nagpur, I felt I had landed at a spiritual oasis. Seeing people being exposed to the Buddha's Dharma for the first time, I thought this must have been what it was like for people to sit and listen to the historical Buddha. I could feel the waves of Dharma spreading from this place in north central India across the sub-continent. I felt grateful to be sitting and sharing company with a diverse Sangha where there is such a renewal of the historical Buddha's spirit. Our instincts for survival tend to drive us into defensive groups with a strong leader. The Buddha's teaching and actions demonstrate that we can grow beyond our instincts for survival by learning to access and follow insights into the deeper nature of the human condition and reality. Deep insight will reveal to us the loving presence of the intimate infinite. This experience allows us to see beyond,

242

gender, caste, race, wealth, education, family of origin and clan loyalty. Transcending these artificial barriers allows us to radically embrace our fundamental equality and the intrinsic worthiness of all beings. I could feel this flowering of realization happening at Nagaloka. A great example of this was manifested in the new relationship I found there with my Dharma brother Rev. Bhante Sugato. He grew up in a Dalit family, converted to Buddhism and then ordained. We kept in contact for a couple of years, but lost touch recently, mainly because of the difficulties of being half-way around the world from each other.

The Nagaloka Center was based on the teachings of Dr. Ambedkar. Before my journey, I read books and saw films about him. Even when he was given a high regional governmental post in pre-liberated India, his subordinate co-workers wouldn't allow him to drink from the same cistern because he was from an "untouchable" caste.

Today many extreme events of abuse and prejudice against the Dalit are reported daily. We have the Black Lives Matter movement here, and in India there has long been a comparable movement, which might be called in English "Dalit Lives Matter." This struggle has been going on since at least the time of the historical Buddha. Still, in much of the country, especially in rural areas, the Dalit are considered "untouchable" and are the recipients of humiliations and physical abuse.

At the campus where I stayed, rural Dalit from around the country came to be educated. It felt a bit like the junior college campus I attended in Los Angeles. More than one student said to me that coming onto campus was the first time in their life that they were treated as human beings. They reported that in their rural village, their families were still excluded from drinking from the village well. They were regularly beaten in the streets for something as simple as walking in front of someone of a higher caste or having their shadow fall across somebody. And, as in the time of the historical Buddha, women especially of a lower caste, were treated more like livestock, to be used and discarded at will. In India today, it's still so extreme. Everything is so stark. For the historical Buddha to accept women and people from the lowest castes into the Sangha was the most radical thing that could be imagined and it is still radical today.

When meeting with Dalit who grew up in the cities, I heard stories which were not as bad. Nevertheless, they all reported discrimination in jobs and advancement. Even professionals from the lower castes still talked about how much prejudice they faced every day. In our country, the amount of prejudice one must face depends a lot on the color of your skin. However, nearly everybody I saw in India had the same skin color. There are no definitive physical traits that reveal the caste you belong to. When in doubt, I'm told, people from the higher castes will ask someone's name because very often the origin of one's name will reveal one's caste. If one's name is associated with a lower caste, they are immediately treated with less respect and subjected to deeply imbedded cultural prejudice.

Prejudice directed at one's gender, sexual orientation, family heritage, geographical origin, disability, religion, skin color is undoubtedly the most insane, stupid kind of painful discrimination we can possibly inflict on each other. Yet, as we are all aware, it's going on throughout the world, all the time. Moreover, from what I have read, there are at least thirty million people who are living the life of a slave today. This is more than at any other time in the history of the planet. These are people who are literally bought and sold. They are kidnapped, manipulated or forced into the sex industry. They are kept as indentured servants. What is it about our species that allows us to treat each other so poorly?

Spiritual practices help us explore our deep nature, and if we manage to do that, we're bound to feel communion with the ground of being that we all share. In the midst of this communion, we can't help but feel an open heart and a loving attitude towards each other. We only need to get past our own defenses, delusions and karmic baggage. It is true that it's easier said than done. Together we must face that we are often caught in our own conscious or unconscious prejudice, preferences, concerns, fears, and dark or conflicted family of origin history.

The conference at Nagaloka was designed to coincide with the annual multi-day memorial of *Dhamma Chakra Pravartan Din* (Mass Conversion Ceremony Day) at the nearby Deekshabhoomi *stupa* (mound-like or hemispherical structure containing relics) honoring B. R. Ambedkar. It was at this site in October, 1956 that Dr. Ambedkar and 600,000 of his followers converted to Buddhism. All the international conference participants, guided and surrounded by the Nagaloka students, joined over a million pilgrims to enter the Stupa and see the remains of Dr. Ambedkar. I've been present at many huge marches and protests in my day; none can compare to joining with a million other pilgrims. A very moving experience to say the least, and I felt that the reverence and respect afforded to Dr. Ambedkar was well placed.

After the conference I went on a guided tour of some of the most revered Buddhist sites. I visited the ruins of Nalanda University, which in its day, 9th Century CE, was the center of Buddhist practice and education in India and the world. I also visited the garden, Venu Vana Kalandakanivapa, where it is said that King Bimbisar provided the Buddha a peaceful park to teach, sit, walk and bathe. I also climbed Vulture Peak, where it is said that the Buddha gave many of his discourses.

The most moving experience was visiting Bodh Gaya
and sitting for an hour under the Mahabodhi Tree where,
it is said, Siddhartha Gautama became enlightened. There
were Buddhist pilgrims from all over the world sitting
there together. I could feel the collective unity, warmth
and interdependence of all beings. While in Bodh Gaya,
my guide also brought me to a rudimentary elementary
school for orphaned or severely disadvantaged children,
VIA Elementary School, which I have been supporting
with a small monthly contribution ever since. The last
place I visited on my pilgrimage was Sarnath, where
tradition says, the Buddha gave his first sermon, revealing
the Four Noble Truths.

Near the conclusion of my journey in India the numbness in my right leg and foot got progressively worse. It was hard to walk, and at one point when I went to get on the back of a motorcycle for a ride, I embarrassingly knocked over the driver and the bike trying to swing my numb leg over the seat. Shortly after I returned to Seattle, in December of 2016, I had a laminectomy to create more space for nerves in the spinal canal. Today my right leg and foot still have some numbness, but I have recovered full functionality of my leg and foot.

BODILY DEPARTURES OF MENTORS AND COMPANIONS

My mother died on October 4, 2017. I was by her side for more than a week, only taking short breaks for meals. At one point towards the end, she asked me why the door in the wall next to her was open. There was no door in that wall. She passed when I briefly left her side for a lunch break. I very much wanted to be with her for her last breath, but, as the hospice nurse explained, people often pass when family members are out of the room. At her request she was cremated shortly thereafter in the Bitterroot Valley in Montana, where she lived only a few blocks from her younger sister.

I wrote the following verse for her that day.

Maureen Dawn O'Shea
7/26/36 – 10/4/17

Early October morning,
the dawn is bright and clear.
At dusk, clouds obscure the mountains
and a soft rain falls.
Eighty-one orbits around the sun in human form,
now a bit of dust and bone.
Who hears the willow's call in a gentle breeze?
Circling over the Bitterroot Valley,
a hawk glides silently, leaving no trace.

Eido Shimano, who was instrumental in building
Dai Bosatsu Zendo Kongo-Ji, died in Japan of pneumonia
on February 19, 2018. He was 85 years old. As I have

related, we first met in Japan at Ryutaku-Ji in 1981 and I actively trained with him from 1996 to 2010. I will be forever grateful for the inspiration he shared about the ancient Zen masters. Despite the great harm he caused to many in his own Sangha and indirectly to me, because I believed his denials, he was one of the greatest catalysts of growth in my life. To this day he remains an enigma to me.

So far I have done five Bearing Witness Retreats. The last one I attended was again at Auschwitz-Birkenau; however, Bernie Glassman was unable to attend because of health issues. On Nov. 4, 2018 all the retreatants learned of Bernie's passing. His wife, Eve Marko was at his side. He was 79 years old. Auschwitz is a depressing place, made even more so by the loss of Bernie. Nevertheless, we all could feel his spirit with us. At Auschwitz-Birkenau no one can hide from just how horrible humans can be to fellow humans. What I learned from this trip was a kind of resignation – collectively it is clear we are not going to evolve any time soon beyond our most primitive instincts to blame, dehumanize and be cruel to others not in our tribe. As much as I will continue to work for progressive causes, peaceful solutions, and a caring approach to all beings great and small, animate and inanimate, perhaps the best any of us can do is to be kinder to each other. Certainly, Bernie would agree and I'm sure he would add that with a caring heart and kind action arising from no-knowing we will have the best chance of surviving our collective adolescence.

On July 29, 2019 the Rev. Kobutsu Malone was found dead in his apartment in Sedgwick, Maine. Kobutsu trained for a time at Dai Bosatsu Zendo Kongo-Ji (DBZ) where I also attended sesshins for many years. Kobutsu's time at DBZ and my time did not overlap, and I am disappointed I never met the man in person; but, he and I became friends after I left the Board of the Zen Studies Society. He was instrumental in Eido Shimano's exposure and downfall through the publication and maintenance of the Shimano Archive. Kobutsu worked tirelessly for the downtrodden and abused, and is well known for his extensive prison work. He was also a woodworker who made nearly every ring found in Chobo-Ji's *rakusus* (the traditional garment worn around the neck of Zen Buddhists who have taken the precepts). Kobutsu was also cantankerous, a chain smoker, and loved guns. He had some serious chips on his shoulders. Nevertheless, I miss our video conversations and I am thankful for his friendship and encouragement over the years. Perhaps our greatest communion together was through our mutual love of dogs. I often wear one of the rakusus he gave me. The most recent was the one he prized, given to him by Shodo Harada Roshi.

Where do we go after we die? I don't know. I do know that our atoms have been orbiting this sun for the last 4.5 billion years and will continue to do so for billions of years more. I also know that those who have been very close or significant to me in this life still live within me, though they are long dead. Moreover, people I've never met but have long read about and studied also feel alive in me. Just to name a few, Jesus, Buddha, St. Teresa of Avila, Meister Eckhart, and many other Christian and Buddhist mystics. From a Buddhist perspective there is no fundamental self to be reincarnated. I've heard the Dalai Lama say reincarnation is of no importance. When asked about reincarnation, I often say, "That's not my sense of reality, my experience is more akin to recycling!" Everything is recycled, and nothing is created or destroyed, except space itself of course, which continues to bloom throughout this ever-expanding universe.

It is ridiculous in my view, to talk about *karma* (the matrix of cause and effect) from past lives being worked out in this life. On the other hand, since we're all intimately and seamlessly connected and the current biosphere incorporates all previous biospheres, we are all working through the karma of previous generations.

All of us are still working out the karma of genocide in Cambodia, Auschwitz, Bosnia Herzegovina, Rwanda, Nanjing and a hundred other places. We are all part of one fabric and endlessly getting entangled and processing each other's karma. I am the product of my Italian great-grandparents who could not survive in Italy and came to America; and the same is true of my grandparents on my Irish side. Their inability to survive in their country of origin, which led to their desperate need to come to America, has had a very real impact on my life. To this day I'm suffering and working through my family's immigration trauma. I'm karmically connected to generations of my family, as you are to yours, and together we must do a better job of processing our collective trauma and the real harm this trauma has brought to this continent and ourselves.

I'm certainly working through my mother's karma

that resulted from being sexually abused as a foster child, and not being able to escape. She had no place else to go; suffering sexual abuse from her foster parents guaranteed that some of that karma would be transmitted to me. My life has long been suffering under the weight of that karma. She's dead now, and I'm still working it out. My father was emasculated in many ways, and he, through his physical and sexual abuse of others, stole masculinity in sick little corners where he could, mostly by beating on his male children and molesting my sister and female cousins. Even though he is long dead, my sister and I are still processing his karma. My brother died a few years ago, so he is no longer suffering. (He was an avid Trump supporter.) The generational madness we have amassed remains for all of us to process. We have neither earned this karma nor deserved it, but here it is, and we must do our best to work it through.

People whose ancestors were enslaved are working through this awful history today. Likewise, descendants of indigenous peoples are still suffering and working through the karmic legacy created when the European settlers invaded this continent. If you look you can feel it. We must share in the suffering caused by our immigrant ancestors and perpetuated by many current government policies. The First Nations are working through their karma brought on by being displaced, eliminated, and culturally decimated. Settlers and those living on ancestral lands must share responsibility to process this collective karma. And, we are adding more negative karma on ourselves by the way we treat new waves of immigrants. We are all seamlessly connected; therefore, for ill or good, we're all collectively working through our karma.

THE PATH OF SPIRITUAL MATURITY

As I have said before, our maturity does not grow like concentric growth rings in the trunk of a tree. Our maturation is more like a growing ameba:

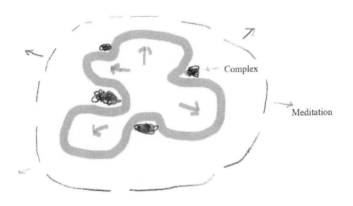

As I see it, growth into adulthood and maturity happens in fits and starts and there are areas of our development that are inhibited and, in some cases, completely arrested by entanglements. Entanglements arise from early wounds or basic needs which are inadequately met in childhood. Carl Jung and others associated with depth psychology have called these kind of entanglements *negative complexes*. As adults we all have areas where we have advanced and other areas where we have not advanced as much. Spiritual practices such as zazen or contemplative prayer help us expand our perception and awareness. This expanding awareness in turn gives us room to grow our skills and mature. It may also shine light on our entanglements and help loosen them up a bit. However, regardless of how much light and spaciousness is gained through meditation or other spiritual practices, it usually will not be enough to dissipate the complexes. Therefore, late in life, even for someone who has had decades of spiritual practice, there may well be negative complexes that are still seriously entangled.

Most, if not all, of us probably recognize that we have some advanced areas of expansion, talent and excellence, along with other areas of soreness, limitation and restriction. If we are unaware of this then it is very likely that our complexes remain in our shadow. When they are unseen and unconscious, these complexes become like boulders in a stream. If the flow of life force and Dharma is strong enough, we may float right over them, but, when the flow is low and strong, (but not so low that the boulders are obvious), they become very dangerous obstacles. If we hit one, we may flip over and drown. If anyone is traveling with us, they may also get hurt or drown. This is how I see three of my deepest mentors, Genki Takabayashi, Joshu Sasaki and Eido Shimano. From the Buddhist perspective all of us are vessels of the Dharma. With a combination of good fortune, lots of natural talent and decades of spiritual practice all three of these men became strong fast-flowing streams of the Dharma. Especially when leading intense weeklong silent retreats, where every participant became raw, vulnerable and therefore more transparent and flowing, the flow of Dharma in these leaders became so massive it hid their boulders of deeply entrenched complexes. At least during the retreats, most people floated right over them, and thought (falsely) that these leaders had no boulders at all.

If these leaders had not done decades of spiritual practice, I don't believe the flow of Dharma, (or Holy Spirit) moving through them would have motivated so many to train with them and fall into the trap of idealization. Unfortunately, many followers were severely hurt when they slammed into their teacher's hidden boulders. Returning to the diagram above, each of these men had some areas of great talent and maturity, and great pockets of stubbornly entrenched arrested development constrained by severely entangled psychological complexes.

Why didn't these men see and address these complexes? Why don't many of us see or address our complexes? For one thing they are often hidden, unconscious and in our shadow. It is impossible to work on them if we are unaware of them. How can we not be aware of them? Most of us compensate our immaturity with our areas of maturity. We can carry the burdensome complexes hidden in our backpack of arrested development. They may slow us down with their weight, but they don't generally interfere with ordinary life and it is only on a long, steep, stressful climb that we are easily exhausted and burdened. At such times we may notice the weight but still be unaware of what we are carrying. In the West we might seek out counseling to investigate the weight we know we are carrying. In the East it is more likely that we will turn to spiritual practices of the ancient masters to find relief. With psychological investigation or analysis, we will likely become aware relatively quickly of what the weight is and where it originated. With continued work, we can then begin the long road of untangling these complexes, processing our wounds and unmet needs, gaining strength and maturity along the way.

Dedicated spiritual practices may well give us relief by lifting us up to lofty vistas far beyond ego entanglements, which may allow our already expansive areas to grow further, but may do little to enlighten us about what the weight is or where it originated. Even if a high vista helps us see a complex, this view offers little assistance in helping us to dissolve or combust the complex. In other words, the relief offered by spiritual practices may only allow us to carry the weight more easily. Spiritual practices that help us carry the weight of knotted-up negative karmic history more easily without combusting or digesting the complexes are a form of spiritual bypassing. Everyone engaged in deeply rooted, heartfelt spiritual practices has experienced some measure of spiritual bypassing. There is nothing wrong with relief, and there is certainly nothing wrong with the growth that is encouraged by expanded perception and awareness. However, unless we turn our view inward and investigate our hang-ups and then dedicate our efforts to loosen, digest or combust them, spiritual bypassing will become a kind of addiction. We can become dependent on it to find relief from the weight of our complexes. And we may become so good at spiritual bypassing that we fool ourselves or our followers into believing that we are spiritually mature!

I was recently asked, is it more useful to be psychologically mature or spiritually awake. There is no question in my mind that being psychologically mature is more useful. I think a psychologically mature person is very aware of both their talents and shortcomings, is on a path of growth and self-mastery, knows how to appropriately care for themselves, and has a deep capacity to see through another's eyes and be empathetic to this suffering world. However, no matter how psychologically mature we may be, if we haven't yet realized and strengthened our seamless intimate connection to beyond the beyond, then we are like a beautiful healthy tree without deep roots. This implies that when there is a personal crisis complicated by multiple planet-wide storms, such as the COVID-19 pandemic, systemic racism and global warming, we will be more likely to break or fall over.

Spiritual practices nurture our roots and help us have access to the sun. Psychological practices work best with everything between our roots and the sun. Of course, a healthy tree needs nurturing on all levels. A healthy tree serves the forest and the world. Every healthy tree is an actualized bodhisattva naturally caring for all beings great and small, animate and inanimate. A tree naturally does its part for the forest, not more than its part and not less than its part. Staying healthy and balanced is the best way to serve the forest of humans and this troubled world. A tree that is sickly or broken, and yet has achieved psychological maturity with deep roots may still serve by being served, or if dead, serve as a nurse log for the next generation of trees. When I'm in hospital, I've learned to caringly allow my caregivers to care for me. When I'm dead I hope that I make a good nurse log both physically and spiritually for the next generation.

The path of maturity does not end with working through the karmic knots of our personal history or with fully realizing our intimate connection to beyond the beyond. These are only the first layers of the onion! The path of maturity is a path of mastery that has no conclusion or arrival at a fixed destination. Wherever we are we are just beginning. This is what is meant by beginner's mind. As long as we have mental acuity, we can continue to explore this vast multi-dimensional universe and deepen our skills for the benefit of all beings. The greatest delusion of all is to think we are separate from others or the environment. Perhaps the greatest crime is to think that we have arrived and have no more work to do. Do other humans have problems? Is the environment healthy and self-restoring? If not then we still have work to do! Yet, it is important not to do more than our part on a given day. When we do more than our share we are interfering with others who are doing their part. We are all different limbs of one body. Moreover, when one of us dies, we all die. When one is born, we are born. When one is enlightened, we are all a bit more enlightened. When one is suffering, we are all suffering. When one of us works on and dissolves, combusts or digests an inner complex, we are all lighter. When our inner negative complexes are not worked on or become more entangled, we are all heavier. The path of maturity requires that we work not only on our personal history but on our collective history, which is full of trauma and entanglements. This crucial work can only go so far if we haven't yet realized our intimate connection to beyond the beyond. Even with full realization, the work of mastery and maturity will stall unless we diligently nurture and strengthen our confidence in communing with the intimate, infinite, subtle but profound presence that animates all universes.

I feel so fortunate to be in a stable, growing, loving long-term partnership. Carolyn and I will complete our thirtieth orbit around the sun together as a married couple in September of 2021, and we were together five years before that. It is my view that if we can tolerate and grow in a long-term intimate relationship together with a fellow human it is the best psychotherapy on the planet. There is no way to be in a long-term intimate relationship and not expose most of (if not all) your complexes to each other. These will naturally flare up from time to time providing an opportunity to process and digest them together, (which assumes the couple has enough skills to do the work). Carolyn and I keep a couples' therapist on call; fortunately, we haven't needed their services for some years.

I have a great appreciation for hermitage and monastic practice; these can be excellent vehicles for awakening to and strengthening communion with the intimate infinite. However, I don't believe that an exclusively monastic training can ever give us all the relationship practice needed to be psychologically mature. Spiritual practice will undoubtedly strengthen our root system and expand our awareness, but without multifaceted relationships outside a monastic setting there will never be enough friction to necessitate turning inward to process our most stubborn karmic shadow material. For this reason, I think cloistered monastic training should be limited to no more than three years and I don't believe it is necessary for the development of spiritual awakening or maturity. Nor do I believe that a long-term stable healthy intimate partnership is necessary for psychological maturity. On the other hand, I'm very doubtful that abstaining from sexual relations throughout one's life can lead to well-rounded psychological maturity. Of course, we all need mentors, guides, and senior companions. Professional counselors and psychotherapists can serve for a slice of this work, but we are too complex for even a great analyst to be our only guide into the dark recesses of our mind.

Whether we see it or not, all people are on the path of awakening, maturity and service. Too often mature enlightenment is confused with traversing the layers of awakening found in the Zen Ox Pictures or the Interior Castle. Mature enlightenment has little to do with multi-dimensional awakening or arriving at final Nirvana. Mature enlightenment is a process of mastery where the "master" never arrives and is always beginning. I've worked with many deeply-awakened individuals who were anything but psychologically mature. And even deeply-awakened psychologically mature individuals may have not yet fully actualized a great vow to be of service to all beings with a caring heart. To have a caring heart does not mean always being sweet, kind and passive. We must realize that all emotions have their place, even fear, anger and guilt. For example, it is appropriate to be afraid of an oncoming train, angry at racism, inequality, brutality and greed, guilty when we take advantage of others for our benefit or hoard our wealth or privilege. In summary, spiritual maturity, the blending of spiritual awakening and psychological maturity, implies walking an endless path of examining this matter of life and death, turning towards our shadow, constantly working to digest or combust our personal and collective entanglements, and coming down from the mountaintop of enlightenment and revelation to work in the market place, kindly lending a helping hand where needed. In my opinion, anyone who tells you they are enlightened isn't. No-knowing is key. A separate, complete self is an illusion. No one needs saving, everyone needs care. How shall we proceed? No-knowing. Let's investigate together.

EPILOGUE

I began this book as the COVID-19 pandemic got started in 2020. None of us knew that a half-million people would die in the United States by February, 2021. The Zen temple where I reside and the Quaker Meeting where I attend shut their doors to in-person public meetings. As with almost all other places of worship, we could only meet through video conferencing. Only a few of the residents at our practice center could practice in person together. Because of pandemic restrictions we could no longer regularly gather in the zendo kitchen to cook vegetarian meals for the homeless; therefore, the temple began contributing financially to our local food bank. We stopped offering quarterly weeklong Zen retreats; however, the temple offered nine Zoom silent meditation sessions a week, a weekly Zoom council, a weekly Zoom Dharma dialogue, eleven Zoom half-day retreats and six Zoom three-day retreats during the year. I would never have guessed that together we could achieve such intimacy and depth using video conferencing. The internet became a much clearer reflection of Indra's Net than I could have imagined.

Beyond the COVID-19 pandemic we are all dealing with the pandemics of polarized and largely dysfunctional political systems, global warming resulting in current and impending environmental disasters, and entrenched systemic racism. That's four pandemics running concurrently.

Recently I was asked how can spiritual companionship help with this multidimensional crisis? Spiritual companions are the best resource possible when it comes to dealing with the fear and the dark nights that we all face from time to time. Spiritual companions provide a bridge from our fear to beyond fear. They offer a mirror to our deep-rooted nature. To paraphrase the Bible, when two or more followers of the Way are gathered together, they can inspire each other to commune with the intimate infinite. For some, our personal fears are amplified by generations of fear instilled in our family tree. Of course, if we go back far enough all humans were more harmonious with nature than we are today. Spiritual companionship can help us recover this harmony with Nature (with a capital "N").

Here in the United States, for the most part we live in a horizontal culture. This nation is less than 250 years old, and we have few generational roots. Because the first peoples to this continent were so decimated by the European invasion, this is even true of our Native American population. Without deep roots we lose our way, and in general do not commune well with Nature.

Therefore, we are all more frightened and blown about by adverse circumstances than we need to be because we are not adequately rooted in something beyond our narrow egoistic view or dominant white tribal view.

In order to be compassionate about systemic racism, first we must have the eyes to see it. If we are white this will require being aware of our innate privilege and natural defensiveness manifesting as white fragility. Only when we can get beyond the fear of losing our sense of entitlement and superiority, will we be able to adequately acknowledge the magnitude of harm still being done as the result of the European invasion of this continent and the importation of enslaved people. Without a deep level of recognition and acknowledgement by the dominant culture it will be very difficult to make the repairs that are necessary to knit our diverse multi-cultural society into a rich and colorful fabric of equity and justice for all. Spiritual Companions can help us to sufficiently fortify our communion with that which best remains nameless. This gives us the grounded foundation to more effectively face and digest our troubled past and work for a more equitable and caring world.

In regards to the COVID-19 pandemic, we have no lived experience of any earlier pandemics, such as the Spanish Flu or multiple bubonic plagues. Our ancestors had no chance of making a vaccine, and many more people died. Humanity somehow survived these events and they were much worse than what's going on now.

Generational memory can sometimes help us in a crisis, but we're too far removed from these earlier collective traumas. The only substitute for a concrete memory of how to deal with the fear, loss and pain associated with these pandemics is, I think, to be spiritually connected to something beyond ourselves.

Our instincts of survival are revved up to high gear by the fears generated by these four concurrent pandemics. Spiritual companionship can help us ground our fear so that it can drain or disperse into the vastness of communion with the intimate infinite. When our fear drains sufficiently to drop out of overdrive, we can begin to make restorative moves towards each other and our planet. If we are not deeply rooted in Mother Earth, we will not be sufficiently motivated to properly care for her. She is messaging us with fires, extreme weather, warmer oceans and increased CO_2 readings, but are we listening? Spiritual companionship brings our heart-minds into alignment so that we may better see through each other's eyes and hear the voice of the planet.

I know no country is a paragon of perfection and all have lots of problems; nevertheless, many countries are doing a far better job than the United States at addressing systemic racism, responding effectively to COVID-19, and cultivating renewable energy sources, all in a less polarized political climate. Canada is far ahead of the United States in restorative justice initiatives with the indigenous First Peoples of the continent. And of course, the United States is not only far behind in addressing Native American concerns, but has barely scratched the surface to address the generational tsunami left by slavery, Jim Crow laws, mass incarceration, and a long societal history of racial profiling. Spiritual mentors help us to cultivate the tools and the spaciousness to process our shadow in such a way that we can make restorative moves for ourselves, our time and our culture. Think of what kind of person you would like to be with in a life-boat far out at sea with only a slim chance of being rescued. Who would you want in that life boat with you? Work in this life to be that person. Spiritual mentors help us to be less anxious in difficult circumstances, to think more clearly during stormy emotions, to sit with and digest our fear. Then, it is easier to be caring and kind to others, even as we die.

Anyone who has had a spiritual breakthrough knows that the greatest gift we can give to another is to share the path and tools for awakening. This led me to ordain as a Zen priest, join a Quaker Meeting, gain a certificate in Spiritual Direction and a Masters in psychology. Along the way I've learned that a path for awakening is only a stepping stone towards maturity. Maturity can only come by processing the joys and sorrows of a lifetime and by facing and digesting the shadow and generational madness we carry. The real beauty of spiritual breakthroughs is that they give us both the foundation and spaciousness, i.e., faith, to do the much harder work of processing our karmic baggage.

Any sufficiently spiritually mature person naturally commits to the great vow to care for all beings. At some point we realize that everyone and everything seen and unseen is an extension of our deep nature, which is not bounded by our narrow idea of self. Therefore, caring for others and the planet is as natural as self-care. A tree cares for the forest by being a healthy tree. My faith prompts me to see everyone as a healthy tree or at least a tree trying to be healthy. As I have said, when I die, I hope my life's journey will be like a nurse log for other trees to grow. If the forest is healthy, it's a loving community by default. In a healthy forest everyone is supporting one another. In a healthy forest the trees commune with all the plants, funguses and animals. If you are standing in a healthy forest you can feel it. Standing in an unhealthy forest, you can feel it. You can sense that something is out of balance or missing. A mature spiritual person is like a skilled, compassionate forester who steadily, over the course of years, works to bring the environment into dynamic balance. A compassionate forester has great patience, knowing change takes time, perhaps many generations. A skilled forester knows that one of their responsibilities is to nurture the next generation of foresters. There is no attachment to outcome because we realize nothing can be saved – not the forest, planet, galaxy or universe. However, in the meantime, it makes sense to protect and nurture our life journey together as best we can.

Whether I'm giving a Dharma interview in the Zen setting, leading Quaker worship sharing, doing one-on-one psychotherapy or offering spiritual direction there is a dynamic, unpredictable, feedback loop process which blossoms in unexpected ways. When I'm in that feedback loop with others, it doesn't matter the context, there's a happening (spontaneous creative activity) that is its own reward. As the dialogue unfolds and deepens, I learn from all the inner sages engaging in the conversation. Sometimes I hear the things coming out of my mouth and I think, "Wow, Genjo you ought to listen to that." The dialogue feedback loop is a kind of cross-pollination where everybody wins. From deep dialogue feedback loops, speaking from the heart and listening from the heart, new revelations and insights arise. When these insights then take root, they will allow our species to move past its adolescence, bringing a greater measure of compassion and harmony to our troubled planet.

ABBREVIATIONS AND GLOSSARY OF ZEN TERMS

Alaya-vijnana: seed repository of consciousness; collective unconscious

AZTA: American Zen Teachers Association

Bodhisattva: Buddhist term for a saint that gives their all for others

Buddha: fully awakened, enlightened being

Chobo-Ji: Listen to the Dharma Zen Temple in Seattle, Washington, the temple where I train

Dalit: untouchable caste in India

Damei: no good, not serving its purpose; useless

DBZ: Dai Bosatsu Zendo and temple in the Catskill Mountains of New York, part of ZSS

Dharma: laws that govern the flow of the universe

Dokusan: brief one on one dialogue with a Zen Master

Dojo: practice hall

Dukkha: suffering, struggle, sorrow, trials and tribulations

FAN: Faith Action Network – Washington state interfaith network for social justice

Gassho: bow with palms together

Karma: the laws of interdependence and causality

Keisaku: waking stick, used to help a student to wake up or become aware

Kensho: sudden spiritual awakening or breakthrough

Kinhin: walking meditation, or any simple motion done with mindfulness

Koan: Zen edicts, tantalizing Zen parables and pithy exchanges between Zen Masters

Kongo-Ji: The name of DBZ Zen Temple

Mu: Japanese ideogram for Emptiness

NYZ: New York City Zendo, part of ZSS

Osho: fully ordained Zen temple priest

PRAG: People's Revolutionary Action Group – a large collective household in Seattle

Rinzai Zen: Japanese Zen school associated with Hakuin Zenji and Rinzai Zenji

Rohatsu: most intense weeklong sesshin in the year, usually the first week of December.

Roshi: honorific title sometimes used for a senior Osho in the Zen Tradition

Samadhi: harmonious state of awareness

Samu: work meditation, usually simple chores done mindfully

Sangha: Buddhist community

Sensei: Japanese word for teacher

Sesshin: a silent Zen meditation intensive, usually a week long

Shobo-Ji: Name of NYZ Zen Temple

Shuku-go: dried karmic dung wedged in one's gut

Soto Zen: Japanese Zen school associated with Dogen Zenji.

Sunyata: Vast Void, alive Emptiness that gives rise to everything

SZC: Seattle Zen Center, precursor to Chobo-Ji, founded by Dr. Glenn Webb

Tao: The Way and flow of Dharma

Teisho: A formal talk on the Dharma usually about a Zen koan

Turning-word: the word in a sentence around which an inquiry is focused

UFM: University Friends Meeting – unprogrammed Quaker meeting in Seattle

Unsui: cloud and water person – novice Zen monk – priest in training

VISTA: Volunteers In Service to America

Zafu: usually round meditation cushion

Zazen: silent seated meditation

Zen: Japanese School of Buddhism that emphasizes seated meditation

Zendo: Zen meditation hall

Zenji: Zen teacher

ZSS: Zen Studies Society which oversees DBZ and NYZ

INDEX OF A PARTIAL LIST
OF SPIRITUAL COMPANIONS

BIBLIOGRAPHY

Saul Alinsky, <u>Rules for Radicals</u>, (Vintage Books) 1971.

Irving Babbitt (Trans.), <u>The Dhammapada</u>, (New Directions) 1965.

David Buerge, <u>Chief Seattle And The Town That Took His Name</u>, (Sasquatch Books) 2017.

Joseph Campbell (Ed.), <u>The Portable Jung</u>, (Penguin Books) 1971.

Sherry Chayat (Ed.), <u>Subtle Sound: The Zen Teachings of Maurine Stuart</u>, (Shambhala) 1996.

Ram Dass & Paul Gorman, <u>How Can I Help?</u>, (Alfred Knopf) 1985.

N. J, Dawood (Trans.) <u>The Koran</u>, (Penguin Books) 1974.

Scott Edelstein, <u>Sex and the Spiritual Teacher,</u> (Wisdom) 2011.

James Fowler, <u>Stages of Faith </u>(Harper & Row) 1981.

Matthew Fox, <u>Breakthrough: Meister Eckhart's Creation Spirituality in New Translation </u>(Image) 1980.

Erich Fromm, <u>You Shall Be As Gods</u>, (Holt) 1966.

Sosan Ganchi Zenji [Chinese: Seng-tsan], <u>Hsin Hsin Ming - Verses on the Faith Mind </u>(Chobo-Ji Sutra Book) 2018.

Glassman & Fields, <u>Instructions to the Cook</u>, (Bell Tower) 1996.

Bernie Glassman, <u>Bearing Witness: A Zen Master's Lessons in Making Peace</u>, (Bell Tower) 1998.

John Gorsuch, <u>An Invitation to the Spiritual Journey</u>, (Paulist Press) 1990.

Donald Grayston, <u>Thomas Merton and the Noonday Demon</u> (Cascade) 2015.

Hakuin, <u>The Zen Master Hakuin: Selected Writings</u>, (Columbia) 2002.

Joan Halifax, <u>Being with Dying</u>, (Shambhala) 2009.

Karen Horney, <u>Our Inner Conflicts</u>, (Norton) 1972.

King James Version, <u>Holy Bible</u> (Collins' Clear-Type).

Philip Kapleau, <u>The Three Pillars of Zen</u>, (Anchor Press) 1980.

Thomas King, <u>The Inconvenient Indian</u>, (University of Minnesota Press) 2013.

Jack Kornfield, <u>A Path with Heart</u>, (Bantam Books) 1993.

D. C. Lau (Trans.), <u>Tao Te Ching</u>, (Penguin Books) 1971.

Brother Lawrence, <u>The Practice of the Presence of God</u>, (Image) 1977.

James Legge (Trans.), <u>The I Ching</u>, (Dover)1963.

Dorothy Lee, <u>Freedom and Culture</u>, (Spectrum) 1959.

Juan Mascaro (Trans.), <u>The Bhagavad Gita</u>, (Penguin Classics) 2003.

Thomas Merton, <u>Zen and the Birds of Appetite</u>, (NDB) 1968.

Alice Miller, <u>The Dharma of the Gifted Child</u>, (Basic Books) 1990.

Arnold Mindell, <u>The Shaman's Body</u>, (Harper Coolins) 1993.

Isshu Miura & Ruth Sasaki, <u>The Zen Koan</u>, (Harcourt Brace Jovanovich) 1965.

Steven Newcomb, <u>Pagans in the Promised Land</u>, (Fulcrum) 2008.
Miklos Nyiszli, <u>I Was Doctor Mengele's Assistant</u>, (Oswiecim) 2010.

Mark Oppenheimer, <u>The Zen-Predator of the Upper East Side</u>, (Atlantic Books) 2013.

Gerard Prunier, <u>The Rwanda Crisis</u>, (Fountain Pub.) 1995.

W. Rahula, <u>What the Buddha Taught</u>, (Grove Press) 1959.

Paul Reps {editor}, <u>Zen Flesh, Zen Bones</u> (Doubleday) 1985.

Joshu Sasaki, <u>Buddha is the Center of Gravity</u>, (Lama Foundation) 1974.

Ruth Sasaki (Trans.), <u>The Record of Lin-Chi</u>, (Institute for Zen Studies) 1975.

Sato & Kuzunisi, <u>The Zen Life</u>, (Weatherhill) 1977.

Sato & Nishimura, <u>Unsui: A Diary of Zen Monastic Life</u>, (China Color Printing Co.) 1982.

Henry Sharman, <u>Records of The Life of Jesus</u>, (Sequoia Seminar Foundation) 1917.

Alan Senauke, <u>Heirs to Ambedkar</u>, (Clear View Press) 2015.

Senzaki, Nakagawa, Shimano, <u>Namu Dai Bosa</u>, (Theatre Arts) 1976.

291

Zenkei Shibayama, <u>The Gateless Barrier: Zen Comments on the Mumonkan</u>, (Shambhala) 2000.

Eido Shimano, Golden Wind, (Japan Publications)1979.

Eido Shimano, <u>Points of Departure</u>, (Theseus-Verlag AG) 1991.

Eido Shimano (Trans.), <u>The Book of Rinzai</u>, (Zen Studies Society Press) 2005.

Jeff Skolnick, <u>Awaken your Brain</u>, (SatoriWest Pub.) 2009.

Huston Smith, <u>The Religions of Man</u>, (Perennial Library) 1965.

Yamakawa Sogen, <u>Selected Teisho on Gateless Gate</u>, (Zen Studies Society Press) 2005.

Marvin Spiegelman, Mokusen Miyuki, <u>Buddhism and Jungian Psychology</u> (Falcon Press) 1995.

Ellen Stephen, <u>A Memoir of the Religious Life</u>, (Morehouse) 2008.

Ellen Stephen, <u>You Really Want to Know?</u>, (self-published) 2018.

Shunryu Suzuki, <u>Zen Mind, Beginner's Mind</u>, (Weatherhill) 1970.

Tanahashi & Chayat (Trans.), <u>Endless Vow: The Zen Path of Soen Nakagawa</u>, (Shambhala) 1996.

St. Teresa, <u>The Collected works of St. Teresa of Avila</u> (Volume Two) (I.C.S.) 1980.

Tich Nhat Hanh, <u>Peace is Every Step: The Path of Mindfulness in Everyday Life</u> (Bantam) 1991.

Tich Thien-An, <u>Zen Philosophy, Zen Practice</u>, (Dharma Publishing) 1975.

Anshin Thomas, <u>At Hell's Gate</u> (Shambhala) 2004.

Brian Victoria, <u>Zen at War</u>, (Weatherhill) 1997.

Benedicta Ward {editor}, <u>The Sayings of the Desert Fathers</u> (Mowbray; Cistercian) 1984.

Glenn Webb, <u>Sugoiyo (OMG)</u>, (self-published) 2015.

Elie Wiesel, <u>Night</u>, (Penguin Classics) 1985.

Yokoi & Victoria, <u>Zen Master Dogen</u>, (Weatherhill) 1976.

Zimmerman & Coyle, <u>The Way of Council – 2nd Ed.</u> (Bramble Books) 2009.

Made in the USA
Middletown, DE
30 October 2022

13755104R00182